# THE MAKINGS OF ME

*My Journey to 7 Figures from My Living Room*

TIFFANY HARRIS

# THE MAKINGS OF ME

Harris, Tifany. *The Makings of Me: My Journey to 7 Figures from My Living Room*



Copyright © 2022 by Tiffany Harris

Published by KWE Publishing: www.kwepub.com

ISBN (paperback): 978-1-942132-04-2



Harris, Tiffany: The Makings of Me: My Journey to 7 Figures from My Living Room

# DEDICATION

**_To my husband Brandon,_**

*This book is dedicated to you, our love, and our relationship. The sixteen chapters honor the sixteen years of friendship we have built. The number sixteen also represents me and my son Cion's birthdate. May 29th equates to 5+2+9=16. This book, like my life, came full circle surrounding the number 16. I love you Mr. Harris I pray for many more years together and growing old together.*
*Love, Your Wife*

**_To my oldest daughter Cianna,_**

*While I know you have been through some things in your young life, know that God got you and that you can get through your struggles but stay prayed up.God will not forsake you nor will he leave you. Understand that life's curveballs will come, but they will never be able to defeat you if you continue to trust in the Lord with all of your mite. Mommy loves you and I will be here for you always.*
*Love, Mom*

**To my son Cion,**

*Continue to stay encouraged son, do not let anyone deter you from your dreams and aspirations in life. Know that I love you and I will always be here for you no matter what. You are a special edition to my life and I am grateful to have you in our family.*
*Love, Your Other Mom*

**To my baby girl Lyric,**

*When you get older you will understand this life a little better but for now continue to keep being you. A loving, caring, kind and gentle person that loves animals and people. I will do my best to teach you everything you need to know in this life. Mommy loves you baby girl.*
*Love, Mom*

**To my family,**

*We all must grow from the trials and tribulations of our lives. I am grateful for each and every one of you. Our trials in life should be looked at as tests that will turn into testimonies later on. We can inspire and uplift one another, therefore, when the time comes that we are physically no longer here our visions and inspirations can live on forever. I love you all.*
*Love. Tiffany*

**To my followers,**

*What would I do without you all? I pray for you all constantly and I hope that the struggles of life will not weigh you down too much. I pray that you will be prosperous in your life's journey. All I can say is to stay steadfast and in prayer because prayer changes things. I love you all and I cannot wait for this book to help you all in your future endeavors.*

*Be blessed, with much love, Tiffany Harris*

# PREFACE: THE MAKINGS OF ME...

It was Sunday, May $29^{th}$, in the great year of 1983 when I was born. Yes, I am an eighties baby. Born in Philadelphia, Pennsylvania, I am from South Philly, $5^{th}$ and Carpenter Street, to be exact. We called my neighborhood "The Pound"! I loved living down $5^{th}$ Street. We had so much fun. I had plenty of friends and family members that lived around or in my neighborhood. I was raised in the church all my life, so I am very religious, and I love, love, love the Lord.

I went to Nebinger Elementary School, and I played the viola. My father was not around much, but I knew who he was. I grew up on food stamps and public assistance, but I was a happy child. My mom was in and out of my life, so I lived with my siblings. I was a good kid, but I got into a lot of fights.

I have five college degrees and a wealth of knowledge to share with others. Hence the reason I wrote this book. This year, 2022, I am now 38 and soon will be 39 years old. I am married to my wonderful husband, Brandon, and we have three awesome children together. My children are my world, and my husband and I work extremely hard to make sure they do not have to go through what we went through growing up without our parents.

I have always been what most people would call a hustler (entrepreneur). When I was young, I would sell items to make money. Throughout my life, I've had the mindset that I needed to make money to take care of myself. I got my first job at fourteen and have been working ever since. It's crazy how life has a way of bringing your past into your present. I wish that I could change some of the decisions I've made in my life, but I do not regret anything.

The Bible says, "She is clothed with strength and dignity; she can laugh at the days to come" (Proverbs 31:25). This is very true for me because I have learned how to look back on my mistakes, evaluate them, and change my route or path before it gets worse.

In the end, if I did not live this specific life, I don't believe I would be where I am today. While reading this book, get ready for the emotional roller coaster called my life. You will cry, laugh, cringe, pray, smile, love, and beg for more, all while also learning the dos and don'ts of business.

This is an entrepreneurial outlook from my view that explores how reality and life do not stop because you have a business. Life will continuously move forward with or without you. I pray that you, the person reading this book, will gain the insight and information needed to succeed in your business and in your life. I wholeheartedly believe that I was placed on this earth to help others, so I wrote this book to help other people not make the same drastic business mistakes I have made.

---

*The Bible says, "Do nothing out of selfish ambition or vain conceit. Rather, in humility value others above yourselves, not looking to your own interests but each of you to the interests of the others" (Philippians 2:3-4). I would say that if you are afraid to step out on faith and take a chance at life, don't be afraid, take the chance anyway. It is okay to fail but you will never be able to succeed if you never try.*

---

## *Chapter One*

# FAMILY DRAMA

***The number 1 represents the beginning! Therefore, this is the beginning of my journey in this life.***

My parents, Marion and Durant, were not married. Actually, my dad was married to someone else. His wife's name was Deborah. I'm not sure if my mom knew about Deborah upfront or if she found out later on. I just know that somewhere along the line, she apparently liked my dad. But later, she developed an extreme hatred for him. Looking back now, I believe that she really didn't know that he was married when they first met.

My mom was very, very popular. She knew everybody and everybody was her "cousin." She'd say, "Tiffany, don't you know so and so? This is our cousin." Everybody loved her. She has a bunch of siblings, too many for me to count. My grandma had ten or eleven kids. The older siblings were pretty much grown by the time my grandma passed away.

When my grandma died from lupus, her younger children went into foster care. As a result, they went through a lot of trauma in their lives. My mom was raped by the next-door neighbor when she was about twelve. From that rape, she got pregnant and had the baby at about thirteen or fourteen.

After the birth, they took the baby from her. My mom went through a lot of mental stress because she knew she had this daughter but had no clue how to get in touch with her. This baby was ripped from her hands. She was just a baby herself, so it was hard on her.

While she never went to nursing school, Mom was in nursing her whole life. She did in-home healthcare and took care of the elderly. She loved what she did.

And Mom loved to cook, too. My favorite dish that she would make for me was beef yock. Instead of going to a Chinese restaurant, she would make it at home. It's basically spaghetti with beef cubes and gravy. At restaurants, the dish has sautéed onions and peppers. Mom knew I hated onions. With recipes that called for onions, she would always make me a separate pot or pan without onions. She would make the beef yock with the noodles, the meat, and the gravy from scratch for me.

Mom also made great soul food, like baked macaroni and cheese, collard greens, and sweet potatoes. She would boil the sweet potatoes and then peel them. I remember her standing at the kitchen sink for hours, pulling out all the strings from the sweet potatoes. It's funny because now I refuse to use real sweet potatoes because I already know I'll be standing there pulling the strings all day. I purposely make sweet potatoes from the can for that reason.

---

My dad was raised in a two-parent household. My grandparents, who are originally from South Carolina, had a nice life. They moved to Philadelphia and had a bunch of kids, too, so my father has a number of siblings as well.

My father was a great singer and was quite a ladies' man. I jokingly called him one of the Temptations because "Papa was a rolling stone..." as the lyric goes.

He was in the Army and served in the Vietnam War. A longshoreman, he worked down at the waterfront with his brothers. He could speak several different languages, including sign language, which he learned in order to communicate with one of his fellow longshoremen who was deaf. And, let's not forget to add that he was also a functioning drug addict.

---

When I was really young, I lived with my mom in Philadelphia, Pennsylvania. My dad lived in the city too, but he lived in a different area, so I didn't see him often. Along with my mom, I lived with my older sister, Shamaine, and my older brother, David, in a two-bedroom apartment. Shamaine is eleven years older than I am, and David is ten years older than me; they are both eighteen months apart. Since I am the baby, my brother calls me Brat.

Oddly, I only have one picture of myself from when I was little. When I asked my family about it, they told me, "Well, in the eighties, parents were more into smoking and drinking and having fun than being worried about taking pictures."

I would say to them, "Okay, that's weird."

In those early days, I remember thinking that my mom was the best mom. She took me everywhere. Every year, she would take me to the circus (Barnum and Bailey or the Ringling Brothers). We always went to see scary movies because we both liked them. She would buy me a cake every year for my birthday, stating that everyone deserves a cake for their birthday. Our birthdays are even eight days apart. So we were really close when I was younger. But that all changed by age ten.

When my brother moved out at fourteen, my mom started putting the responsibility for caring for me on my sister. Anywhere my sister went, I had to go, even though she was eleven years older than me. Here was my sister at fourteen years old walking around with her three-year-old sister. I believe she really disliked it, but she knew better than to go against what my mom said.

By the time I turned eight and my sister was twenty, there was an even greater shift between me and my mom. She started leaving me with my sister all of the time, saying, "Hey, I need you to watch her. I'll be back." And then, she would leave for weeks on end. When Mom did appear, it was usually because she needed a place to stay. In Philly, if you needed to go into a shelter, you had to have children. My mom would pick me up from my sister's house and take me to a shelter so that she would be able to have a place to stay. That meant that I jumped around with her from shelter to shelter, and I switched schools a lot back then.

I didn't have a real relationship with my father because of the situation with him and my mother. I remember once being with my mom in a shelter down the street from my father's house. I remember thinking that he had this whole house.

*Why are we in this shelter? Why won't he let us come and stay with him?*

I'm not sure if he didn't offer to let us stay with him or if he did and my mom decided not to accept. I do remember that I caught the bus to go to school right at the corner of his house.

When I turned ten, my sister said to my mom, "You always bring her here and leave for long periods of time. So why don't you just leave her here?" And that was the beginning of my sister taking custody of me without actually legally taking custody.

My sister had a best friend, Tatrina, that my mom took in because her mom was in jail, so she lived with us, too.

My mom was great with helping people and she loved to do it. When I was seven, my best friend Janine lived a few doors down with her grandma. My mom took in Janine like she was one of her own. Janine and I did everything together, and she was always very overprotective of me. She would fight everyone and we kept getting into trouble. When you saw her you would see me. We were so close that everyone thought we were sisters so that title stuck; now we are sisters forever. While we don't get to see much of each other or hang out like we used to, I love my sister. When we do get together it's like we never missed a beat.

Shamaine, Tatrina, and David, my three older siblings, did everything for me. Shamaine boughtall my clothes, David bought all my sneakers, and Tatrina would do my hair in all the different styles of the 1990s that everybody wanted and had. I would see my mom whenever she decided to pop up in our lives.

One of my dad's brothers lived on the same block as my house. We called him Uncle Tree because he's really tall. As I grew up, if I needed anything, I would just go to Uncle Tree. I could literally just go to his house and ask, "Uncle Tree, can I have two dollars for lunch?"

He would give me five dollars and then say, "Don't spend it all in one place."

Even with Uncle Tree and my brother David around, I never felt like I had a father figure. That role was just nonexistent in my life. The same was true about having a mother role model. Shamaine didn't play the role of my mom when my mom wasn't around. I was alone, and I just did what was needed or what was asked of me.

From age ten through high school, life was difficult. Shamaine was in a marriage, and I really disliked her husband. It was tough for me to stay in a household with them because he was hard to deal with.

Because of this, I would often stay at my ex-boyfriend's house with him and his mom, Towanda. I met him when we were twelve at a family cookout. My sister Tatrina and his cousin Meeka were best friends and would throw a family get together annually. Then one year we met and it was seemingly love at first sight. We would talk on the phone all night long. One day I decided to sneak up on him and show up unannounced at his house. His mom answered the door. She was a beautiful woman and she was dressed really fly. When I knocked on the door and she answered I asked if her son was home. She said, "No, may I ask who's asking?" I stated my name was Tiffany and she immediately smiled really big and said, "Oh my God! He talks about you all the time! Come in, sweetie." I was nervous but I obliged and from that point on we were really close, Towanda and me.

And then, in January of my ninth-grade year, my dad was murdered. But we'll talk about that later.

---

*"The Lord is good, a refuge in times of trouble. He cares for those who trust in Him" (Nahum 1:7). I was not a child that grew up with a silver spoon. I grew up with the understanding that it is better to have Jesus than silver and gold.*

---

*Chapter Two*

# IF FAMILY DRAMA WASN'T ENOUGH, LET'S ADD SOME HEALTH ISSUES

***The number 2 represents harmony, balance, and love. It is also a symbol of your mission in life and what you were placed on this earth for. It symbolizes trust and faith. Number 2 is sometimes used to test your patience.***

Since my family was religious and we believed in the Resurrection, Easter was a huge holiday for us. We always prepared for it with nice hairstyles and beautiful dresses and by attending church. Easter Sunday, March 26, 1989, was a day I will never forget.

I was six years old. My mom was doing my hair. We were at the kitchen sink. I was sitting in a chair and my mom was standing over me, using a hot comb on the stove to straighten my hair out.

When moments later my head fell into the sink, my mom kept saying, "Lift your head up." And then, after she kept asking, "Why are you doing that?" she realized that something was wrong. She put the hot comb down and then she tilted my head back towards her.

She saw my eyes roll into the back of my head. She immediately knew to put me on the floor, on my side. And by the time she had placed me there and I had started to seize, she called 911. Needless to say, I didn't attend church on that Easter Sunday. That was my first seizure, and seizures were ongoing from there.

Later, I learned that my mom had epilepsy as well, so it may have been hereditary. They're called partial seizures now, but back then, they were called grand mal seizures. My mom had those too.

My second seizure happened when I was twelve. It coincided with me getting my period. At the beginning, it would happen once a month, sometimes once every six weeks. After that, I kept having horrible seizures.

One time, I was rushed to the ER in middle school, around eighth grade. When I had this seizure, I fell down a flight of steps at school.

When I arrived at the ER, I guess I was bigger than what the doctor expected a fourteen-year-old to be. He sized me up and gave me an adult dose of seizure medicine without testing me first. And I had a severe allergic reaction to it. However, we didn't know I was having a reaction at first.

About two weeks after being sent home from the ER, I got an early dismissal from school because I had a doctor's appointment. My mom picked me up from school and we went to Jefferson Hospital to go see my neurologist. I remember sitting on the little doctor's bed in his office while he was asking me questions.

"What year is it? Who's the president?" he quizzed.

At first, I was answering, and then I stopped.

He was standing in front of me and he kept asking, "Who's the president?"

I was staring off into space. And then my mom said, "Oh, no, I think it's about to happen again."

He asked, "What?"

As he turned around to say something to her, I passed out, fell off the bed, and hit the floor.

Then the neurologist immediately shouted to the nurse, "Call 911!" He tried to put a pillow under my head and rolled me on my side. I had a seizure right in front of him.

Since I seized in his office, the neurologist was able to see what happened. This was a blessing because all of the tests he and his associates ran on me kept coming back negative or inconclusive. As a result, they thought I really wasn't having seizures. The doctor, seeing it happen in front of him, admitted me to the hospital.

My mom told the neurologist the name of the medication I was on. It was Dilantin; I will never forget it.

He stated, "Let me go get her records."

Because this was in the 1990s, before electronic records, everything was on paper. He found the medication that I was on and discovered that the dosage was too high.

He told my mom, "I'm going to admit her to the hospital."

That's when they started to figure out I was having an allergic reaction to the Dilantin.

The doctor at the hospital said, "She's been given way too much daily. It's going to take a while to get it out of her system."

They decided to give me an antibiotic to help. But I'm not that easy, and neither is my body.

The antibiotic they decided to give me, penicillin, was not working. And soon we found out that I was allergic to that as well. To this day, we still don't know if it was the Dilantin or the penicillin that caused my kidneys, liver, spleen, and gallbladder to be affected.

Altogether, I was in the hospital for two months. During the first month, they were trying to figure out some kind of concoction to bring down the allergic reaction and stop the inflammation in all of my organs.

It was during the second month that they said, "Okay, we need to get a specialist in here because this is way over our heads."

Whichever medication caused the trouble, it affected many of my organs, and I almost died.

I lived because God guided the doctors to bring help. They brought in a specialist from Japan who was working on a trial dealing with children with epilepsy. These specialists did a bunch of different surgeries on me. They had to take out my lymph nodes because they swelled up so badly that I couldn't breathe on my own.

They gave me a skin graft on my arms. They took little pieces of my skin and tested the different medications before they gave them to me after my initial reaction. I still had reactions, however.

My eighth grade year was horrible. Due to the allergic reaction, my first layer of skin fell off, and all of the skin on my whole body became very flaky and ashy. I thought it would just about kill me because it hurt so badly. My skin would peel off. Tatrina would get different creams and mix them all together to make elixirs. She would wipe them all over my entire body every day.

People teased me, calling me Ash Wednesday and other mean things. When my sister started rubbing the creams on me, people would call me a grease monkey because my skin was super shiny. But thankfully today I have nearly perfect skin, so all of that may have been worth it. (Silver lining!)

Once I was hospitalized, the seizures began occurring weekly, sometimes a couple of times per week.

Once, I had to get an EEG. I had to wear gear on my head for a whole weekend. I was so embarrassed because I had to get on public transportation with this equipment on my head while carrying the machine. Every time they did these tests, they never learned why the seizures were happening. The tests would always come back as negative or inconclusive.

The medical professionals would tell me, "Oh, well you know red meat is bad for you if you have seizures, you've gotta stop eating red meat. Oh, you've gotta stop drinking Sprite. Oh, you gotta blah, blah, blah…"

Meanwhile, I was lost saying, "What?"

We would do all those things, avoid those foods and beverages, and still I would continue to have seizures.

Eighth grade year was hard because there was a lot of bullying, a lot of teasing. For example, I remember this one time I came to school. I believe it was Easter Monday as I was dressed up really cute with a new outfit and new shoes. One of my classmates told me that she liked my shoes. Another classmate screamed across the room, "The shoes are cute, but she's ugly and ashy!" Everybody laughed.

Every time I would get my period, I would have a seizure. The school realized that this would happen every month.

In high school, I fell down steps and hit my head a few times. The principal said, "Okay, we can't do this. We'll send her work home." The principal told my mom, "She's going to have to stay home during the week of her period."

And it didn't stop until I was about twenty-two years old. That's when I had my last seizure. To this day, they still do not know why I had them or why they stopped. But the great thing is I no longer have them.

Then came my next sickness busting through.

When I was seventeen I had my first asthma attack. I

thought I had the flu or a cold. One minute I was fine and the next minute I could not breathe. I told my mom, "Something's wrong." She started asking me questions, and I became really irritated, insisting, "I'm telling you I can't breathe!"

She called 911, and when they came, the paramedics gave me oxygen. When I got to the hospital I received my first nebulizer treatment. They decided to give me a medicine called Prednisone, a steroid, along with an Albuterol inhaler.

This wasn't new to me because my sister, Shamaine, had really bad asthma. I spent my whole life watching her when she had attacks. As time went on, we realized that I had something different from Shamaine, I have allergy-induced asthma.

Now, it hits me seasonally when the seasons change. However, I never had a break because I would have asthma attacks throughout the whole year. I am allergic to every season!

I wound up obtaining a home nebulizer machine. I was on many different steroid medications during the changing of the seasons. Luckily for me, asthma slowed down, at least until I moved to Virginia.

Most of the time, it felt like a really bad cold or the flu. In the spring I would have asthma attacks where I couldn't breathe. It closed up my airways. In the summer, in addition to being unable to breathe, I had nosebleeds. I would wake up in the morning and there would be blood everywhere from my nose. In the fall, my symptoms would be a little sketchy. I could get the spring-like asthma symptoms and flu-like symptoms. And then in the winter, I would get pneumonia.

I started receiving allergy shots three times a week, and continued to do so for a very long time. I got allergy shots for about five years straight until I became pregnant with my baby girl.

My doctor said, "We can't give you these shots while you're pregnant."

After that, I didn't go back. And fortunately, I have not had an asthma attack since.

My health issues messed up everything. I got a full-time job at sixteen at Wendy's, working there after school. Sometimes I would have seizures at work. Sometimes I would have an asthma attack.

The good part about that Wendy's was that I worked directly across the street from Jefferson Hospital. If I had an attack, my coworkers would call the hospital and say, "Y'all need to come over here and get her!" They would tell my mom to come and sign some paperwork because I was at the ER for a seizure or asthma attack.

The health issues impacted my personal life, too. I first received my driver's license when I was twenty while I was in college. As we say at Penn State University, WE ARE...PENN STATE! About two years later, while living and working in Delaware, I was employed at a clothing store. As I was leaning over to pick up some clothes off of the dressing room floor, I had a vertigo spell, and then I went into a seizure. So the state of Delaware took my driver's license for six months. I had to be seizure-free for six whole months before they would give it back.

After they gave my license back, I became afraid to tell people that I had seizures. I was scared the state would take away my license again. I avoided telling new employers about my conditions as they wouldn't want to hire me if I told them.

Eventually, I realized when I'm getting ready to have a seizure, I might feel dizzy and I usually have an aura. That way, I could tell when it was getting ready to happen. For the most part, my auras were really scary but cool. I would blink, and then it appeared as if the ceiling was on the floor and the floor was on the ceiling, but I was still standing straight. Then, I would tell my coworkers, "Y'all are going to have to call 911. I'm about to have a seizure." And then, I would just lay on the floor.

Sometimes when I would get the aura, vertigo would kick in and I would pass out. That's what happened whenever I would fall down.

When I was fourteen or fifteen, I got the cartilage of my ear pierced. I was trying to take one of the earrings out because it was hurting me. As I was trying to get it out, I had a vertigo spell, passed out, and hit my head on my bunk bed. My two bottom teeth went through my top lip, and then I had a seizure.

I started to put together patterns. Your ears have many nerves that can cause vertigo. The vertigo made me pass out. And after passing out, I would have an epileptic fit. I had to experience these different stages before realizing all these things were connected. Once I realized the patterns, I started to avoid the triggers.

I never got my ears pierced again. It was hard as a teenager because there were things I wanted to do but had to avoid because I was too afraid that something would happen.

One of my biggest triggers is strobe lights. To this day, I still cannot be in direct contact with strobe lights or I will have a seizure. I stay away from nightclubs or parties that have anything really bright and flashy. Those are all triggers. I'm like, "Stay away from the light, Carol Ann," like the movie *Poltergeist*!

During the whole four years I was at Penn State, I had four or five seizures. I had started to piece together that my seizures were also stress-related. If I got too stressed out, I would have a seizure.

I remember feeling like I was about to have a seizure at one of the parties at school. We had a Halloween party in the multipurpose room. It wasn't a really big room as I went to a branch campus of Penn State. At this party, there were strobe lights, and I was there dancing and having a good time.

Then, I started to feel the floor and the ceiling swap, and that let me know to get out of the room. I just was like, "Okay, I'm gonna walk away." I told one of my friends, "I'm really dizzy."

I went and I sat outside in the cold, on the curb, trying to get my bearings back, and I actually did not have a seizure. From that point on, I just tried to be more conscious about what I was doing, where I was at, and who I was with.

The next seizure scare I had in college was when I had to get my wisdom teeth surgically removed. The doctor gave me Vicodin, and apparently my body didn't like that as I had an allergic reaction to it. And I had a seizure. I couldn't talk, I had tampons in my mouth—yes, y'all, OB tampons—in my mouth to catch all the saliva, and to make matters worse, I was having a seizure.

Can you just picture the paramedics trying to get tampons out of my mouth while I'm grinding my teeth from having a seizure? Oh, my God. I was clenching down on them while I was having a seizure. When I have a seizure, I can hear everything people are saying, but I can't respond. I could hear everybody talking, what they were saying, who was scared, and who was crying. I could hear all of that, but I couldn't respond. When I would come back, I would think, *Okay, Tiffany, you're gonna have to have a conversation with so and so because she was really scared.*

People would be afraid to be around me. That was hard because it was my first year at college. I was meeting people and when they found out I had seizures, they were either going to be really sympathetic to me, you know, like babying me, or they would be like, "Oh, no, I can't be around her."

I dealt with more days in the ERs and the hospitals from having seizures than I did from asthma, but I saw more doctors because of the asthma. The doctors were puzzled about why my asthma onset came so late. It was later that they realized I had allergy-induced asthma. Like most people with allergy-induced asthma, I also have eczema.

If I get sick and I have to go to the doctor or the hospital, the first thing I tell them is "don't give me that" when they try to prescribe medication. The only time I go to the doctor is when I find myself sick to the point of dying. They are most likely going to give me something that I'm allergic to anyway.

That happened when I was in the hospital in 2021. I had a hysterectomy, and I was only supposed to be there overnight. The next day, I went home, and everything seemed okay. The day after that, I started bleeding uncontrollably. We were trying to figure out why I was bleeding since they took out everything that technically makes a woman bleed.

It was just my luck that I had an allergic reaction to the antibiotic, and I wound up having an infection in my blood. I became septic (and almost died again). My one overnight stay in the hospital for this surgery wound up turning into twelve days in the hospital.

I don't have any luck when it comes to medications or surgeries, but I always make it out alive. I don't take too much of anything these days out of fear. I feel like my body doesn't like me like I did something wrong to my body in a past life and it's just not here for me anymore. But then, I sit back and I think about how God has made it possible for me to still be alive through all of those things. I'm grateful for that. And then, I can't hate my body but so much.

I went through a lot of hard years of sickness, and to be

able to say that, even though I went through all those tough times, I haven't had any health issues lately and that is a great thing. I've been seizure- and asthma-free for seventeen plus years.

It's a gift from a curse.

---

*"I can do all things through Christ which strengthens me" (Philippians 4:13). A wise woman once told me, "Life will HUMBLE you if you don't believe me keep LIVING! (Towanda Johnson)*

---

*Chapter Three*

# MY FIRST HEARTBREAK

***The number 3 represents wealth, whether that is in knowledge or financially. It also represents the Holy Trinity in the Bible. The number 3 represents creativity and the ability to express one's emotions.***

The day my father died, it was his birthday, January 8, 1998. He had a party, a little get-together, at his house. Someone shot him in his legs and hit a major artery. He bled out. Whoever did it wrapped him up in a carpet and set him out on the sidewalk like he was trash. He was found because some construction workers went across the street to eat their lunch. One of the construction workers kicked the carpet and a pair of feet fell out. After that, my father sat in the morgue for about three weeks.

During that time, no one posted his picture or shared that there was a missing person. They never said anything on the news. Nothing ever happened. The truth was uncovered because my father was a longshoreman. Even though he was a functional drug addict, he went to work faithfully every day. And when he didn't come to work for three weeks straight, all of his brothers down at the waterfront were feeling like, "Something's up. We need to find him." Even after someone told my uncle to go and check the morgue, he waited for a little over a week before he decided to go.

When my uncle did end up going to the morgue, he identified my father's body. By then, my father was starting to decompose. We had to get a funeral set up quickly, but that was harder than it sounded. My father had a wife in Rhode Island, and he had a child over there. He had me, and then he had other children with other women around the city of Philadelphia. Pulling everyone together to have this funeral was a big project.

Shamaine and David didn't like my dad, so they didn't attend his funeral. They always said he was mean, and they remembered when he and my mom were together because they're older than I am. I think my dad beat my brother, and after that, he never liked him again.

On the day of his funeral, I was surprised to meet five of my seven sisters, Colette, Katrina, Dominique, and Chrystal. I also met my step-sister, Elisha, that day. (I met my other step-sister, Leandra, later.) Before that day, I had no clue that they even existed. All of our moms knew each other, and they knew that they all had children by this man, and yet they never said anything to any of us.

The silver lining to the dark day of my father's funeral is that we are all really, really close now; I keep in contact with most of my siblings. The exception is my oldest sister, whose name I don't know, because she didn't show up to the funeral. We don't know her at all, not her name or anything about her. This means I have two sisters that I have never met, and probably never will, unfortunately.

---

Prior to his death, my dad's wife, Deborah, decided she was going to move away to Rhode Island because he was abusive to her. At the time my father was murdered, officials contacted her because they were still married. She came down to Philly and did whatever she needed to do for his funeral. Her plan was not to return. My two younger sisters, Dominique and Chrystal, are eighteen months apart in age. On the day I met them at my father's funeral, they were five and six years old. We call Dominique Diamond, and we call Chrystal Cece.

Cece hid behind her mom and was peeking out.

Their mom, Elaine, said to her, "This is your older sister, Tiffany."

I met Elisha at my dad's funeral too, when she was only two. Elisha is Diamond, Cece, and Trina's younger sister and Elaine's fourth daughter. She's not my father's child, but because she's so close in age to Diamond and Cece, I consider her to be my little sister too. She would always tag along with us anywhere we went.

My sister, Katrina, and I are a little bit closer in age. I call her Trina. She took me under her wing, and we would go on all kinds of adventures together. We went to Jamaica when I was eighteen. Another time, we took a Greyhound from Philadelphia all the way to New Mexico. The whole trip took forty hours on the bus! While it was long and tiresome, Trina and I had a great time. Once we arrived in New Mexico, we could walk out of our hotel and across a bridge and we would be in Mexico. All we had to do was show our birth certificates. This was a time before you needed a passport to go across the border.

Since Trina and I were so close, I was often at their house. As a result, I became closer with her mom, Elaine. She would tell me about my dad, and I would always continue to ask her stuff. "What was he like? What would he do? What would he say?" And she would tell me. From Elaine, I learned that my dad loved to sing and what his favorite song was.

Elaine was very open about sharing information about him with me. I would ask questions and then she would just sit down and talk with me. That's why I found it really odd that she wouldn't tell her own children about him. It was up to me to retell the information that I was told to my siblings. Even to this day, my younger sisters reach out to me and ask me questions about my father.

From the time that Diamond was about nine and Cece was about eight until they were teenagers, we would go together to visit my father's grave. I believe out of all the years that he's been gone, we are the only three who have visited him.

When I would take my little sisters, we could never find him because he didn't have a tombstone. We would go to the cemetery office and they would always give me a map. They would put an "X" over top of Barbara Edwards. Her tombstone was on the other side of my dad. Barbara Edwards had a really nice tombstone; you couldn't miss it.

Before we would visit his gravesite, I would plan different things for Diamond, Cece, and I to do. On Veteran's Day, we would go to the Dollar Tree and purchase little American flags to place on his grave. Sometimes, we would bring little fake flowers. Since I attended a vocational high school, I always made clay and other artwork to bring, especially because he didn't have a tombstone. Every time, however, the groundskeepers would move what we left. It's sad that the groundskeepers would move it, but I guess that was their job.

I knew I had to figure out a new plan for remembering our dad. When Diamond, Cece, and I would visit, I began telling them different stories or memories that I had of my father. I told them how he would ask me to roll up all the change, putting pennies into rolls, and then take them to the corner store to get the money for my lunch at school. My sisters were so young that they didn't know him. Granted, I didn't really know him either, but I at least had some activity with him. They don't remember anything about him.

I talked to my stepmom, Deborah, and shared that when I would take my younger sisters to go visit my father at the graveyard, we couldn't find him.

She asked, "What do you need to do to get the tombstone?" I was only sixteen at the time, so I couldn't really do anything.

Basically, she just flat out told me, "I would not have a problem with you guys getting a tombstone for him, but I'm just not gonna be a part of it."

Over the four years after my father passed, my sister, Colette, and I would talk on the phone and write letters to each other. When I turned eighteen, I visited Colette. I traveled by bus to visit her in Rhode Island so that I could attend her college graduation. She graduated from Rhode Island College and got her bachelor's degree in nursing and became a registered nurse.

Leandra is Colette's younger sister. She's not my father's daughter, but because her mother was married to my father, she's my stepsister. I actually didn't meet her or even know anything about Leandra until I came to Rhode Island for that visit for Colette's graduation.

During that trip, I stopped at the cemetery and requested the paperwork for a tombstone. Because my father was a veteran, he technically could get a free one. Well, not completely free, but we just had to pay the $50 application fee. I had the money, but I couldn't sign off because Deborah was still his wife. During that trip to Rhode Island, I asked her to sign the paperwork. To my surprise, not only did Deborah sign the paper, but she actually wrote me a check for one hundred dollars to get a tombstone.

Six months later, they put his tombstone up. My little sisters and I didn't have to look for Barbara Edwards anymore. We could just go directly to his tombstone. That was pretty cool.

Once we finally got the tombstone for Dad, Diamond, Cece, and I went a few more times. By that time, since I was eighteen, I went to college, so I wasn't able to take them as much. Since every single last one of our moms hated him, it wasn't like Elaine was going to take them to Dad's gravesite. The situation with the tombstone helped. I just felt so accomplished because no one had to look or search for him like we did.

---

Colette and I continued to remain close. I actually wound up moving in with her for about four months after I had my daughter, Cianna. While I don't talk as often with Elisha and Leandra, they know that if they need to talk or they need me for something, I'm here for them.

I wanted to know about my dad because he was my dad. Whether I knew him or not, I felt that loss; I lost a parent that day, and it was a hard pill to swallow. And I remember feeling some type of way. When my dad was murdered and we found out, I cried.

My sister Shamaine asked, "What are you crying for? You

didn't even know him."

That hurt me. I said, "I'm crying because without this man, I wouldn't be here."

It's heartbreaking that I didn't know him. When I felt like I had the opportunity to get to know him but, it was taken away from me.

However, I felt like it was like a blessing from God that, even though I didn't get to know my father, I got to know my siblings.

Shamaine and David have their own fathers, so they have their own set of siblings as well. All of us are pretty close now. I had temporary custody of Diamond when she was a teenager, so my siblings from my mom's side are close with Diamond because she lived with me. Colette, Shamaine, and I are close as well. David has two brothers from his dad, and I consider them to be my brothers. Even though their dad is not my dad, we are all family no matter what. It was weird at first, and now? Now it's normal.

My sisters on my dad's side and I decided that we wanted to break the generational curse that our parents laid out for us. As we began to get older and have kids, we decided we wanted to make sure that our children knew each other. We got together and went on a vacation to Florida with our children. We don't want to create a stigma the way it was with our parents, where we actually had blood-related siblings and yet we didn't even know we existed.

---

***"The Lord is my shepherd; I shall not want. He maketh me to lie down in green pastures: He leadeth me beside the still waters. He restoreth my soul: He leadeth me in the paths of righteousness for His name's sake" (Psalm 23:1-3). If it doesn't challenge you, it will not change you.***

---

***The number 4 represents self-expression, mental well-being, and contentment.***

Growing up, I hated school because I was always being teased. In elementary school, I was bullied and picked on. I fought a lot, and I was jumped a lot. I used to get bullied all the time until one day I decided to fight back. That was the beginning of a long, draining, and seemingly never-ending cycle. I fought almost daily. Eventually, I was expelled from Nebinger Elementary in 8th grade and went to Pierce Middle School for the remainder of my eighth-grade year. Pierce was a great school; I loved it—no fighting, just learning and having fun.

Since I enjoyed my middle school, I purposely chose a high school that was not in my area so I wouldn't go to school with the same people from my elementary school because all I did was fight with them.

As a result, I loved high school. I was popular. It was like a turn of events. And since I was smart, I was able to go to an academic vocational high school. I did have to travel a ways to get there, but it was probably the best decision I could've made. I made lifelong friends. I'm still close with everyone that I was close with in high school.

Everybody knew who I was. I was student government president, I sang in the choir, and I played volleyball and basketball. High school was way better than elementary and middle school for me. High school made me feel like I belonged somewhere.

In my actual life, I didn't feel like I actually had a place to belong because my dad didn't want to be bothered. My mom didn't want to be bothered. My sister was busy working, and my brother was incarcerated.

When we were 15 Janine got pregnant and had a baby. My godson Jaquil (boo boo is what Jaquil and I call each other) was the most precious baby boy with the most beautiful gray eyes. It was love at first sight for me. I was right there with my sister Janine when she gave birth. This was a moment in my life that I will never forget. But for some reason I still felt like I was alone. Everyone had someone to love them but me was how I felt.

When I went to high school, I felt like, “Well, I have these new friends and they seem pretty cool, so I guess I'll give them a try.”

I chose to get into choir and volleyball because I wanted to be a part of those activities. They kept me occupied, and I didn't have to go home and be bored. It’s funny because I don't think any of my friends in my group did any of those things. I joined volleyball, basketball and badminton teams because we would go on trips to other schools to compete. I wasn't even good at any of them.

You might think I would have a hard time playing sports since I had epilepsy. That wasn't the case. Having the seizures gave me an excuse so I did not have to take gym class, and everybody would get mad, making statements to me like, "How are you on all the sports teams, but you can't go to gym?" All I had to do at first was just put on my gym uniform. As long as I was present, I got a passing grade for gym. I could play sports until I had a seizure, then the school would prevent me from playing due to medical reasons. Because of this, I never played a full season.

Once I was elected to the student government, the teacher who presided over the Student Government Association (SGA) realized that I was smart and I could do different things. Dr. Hightower would give me tasks and as I got them done, she started letting me go to her class during my gym time. I grew a close bond with Dr. Hightower, she was an awesome mentor and something like a mother figure to me sort of like my school momma.

And then she died from breast cancer—and I was crushed.

My mom did go with me to her funeral, which was in New Jersey. It was about an hour away. I had a friend in the automotive shop who knew how to drive. He drove me and my mom over to the funeral. By the time we got there, however, they had already closed the casket. So we missed the viewing. While I was upset about that, I was at least able to go to her funeral and say goodbye. I was also able to meet her daughter whom she spoke a lot about to me. I found out that she also spoke highly of me to her daughter as well. That warmed my heart in that moment and taught me to appreciate the people that God brings into your life because they are here for a reason, season, lesson, or blessing.

The next person who took over the SGA was Mr. Murphy.

At first, I felt like, "I don't want a man to do this position. I want it to be a woman so that we can talk and she'll understand me."

But Mr. Murphy, he talked with me. He treated me like I was his daughter. You could say he was my school dad.

Mr. Murphy was my new backbone. He helped me during my bad senior year, during which my boyfriend and I broke up and he went to jail. I got sexually assaulted during that year. I had a seizure as I was getting ready for the prom and another seizure on the day of my graduation. I almost didn't graduate because I refused to go to chemistry class. It was boring and too early in the morning, so I was late many days. The only reason why I passed chemistry is that my teacher had a crush on Mr. Murphy.

To help me, Mr. Murphy decided he would reach out to my chemistry teacher to discuss some options for me to get a passing grade. She told him if I submitted a science project to the science fair and took her on a date, she would give me a passing grade. Can you imagine what it would have looked like for the class SGA President (me) to fail 12th grade? Mr. Murphy took one for the team and took her on a date. I completed my portion of the deal and entered my color wheel science experiment into the fair. She gave me an A!

I remember Mr. Murphy saying, "Now that you're going to actually graduate, what do you want for graduation?"

As the student government president, they were planning to call me up on stage and present me with something. I was joking with him, and I said, "I want a big trophy for all my hard work."

And he bought me the biggest trophy; I still have it on my bookshelf.

I was the first of my mother's children to go away to college and live on campus. During my entire senior year of high school, representatives from different colleges would come and ask for me by name. I did not want to talk to them. I would avoid them.

I hated school. I didn't like schoolwork. I didn't want to do it.

Before then, I wanted to go to Spellman. That became my dream. I used to watch *A Different World,* the spinoff of *The Cosby Show*. The college on their TV show was like a cross between Spellman and Morehouse. I was then dead-set on going to Spellman. It wasn't until I got into 11th or 12th grade when I realized, *Oh, you need a 4.0, so how am I going to get into there?*

That is when I decided I just did not want to go to college at all—until I realized that it may have been my only option. So, I signed up and started my college journey.

---

***" Lord, how excellent is Thy name in all the Earth! Who has set Thy glory above the heavens?" (Psalm 8:1). It was then that I realized my strength and that no matter what nothing would ever hold me back. I am going after everything that is for me.***

---

# HAPPY VALLEY

***The number 5 represents curiosity and adventures.***

Just because you attend college doesn't mean you're going to get a job!

When I was in high school, Penn State recruiters came to my school, literally every day, trying to recruit me. I was like, "Nope, I don't wanna go. I don't wanna go. I don't wanna go." I just wanted to be done with school. I hated school. I've always had seizures, and then asthma came, and then it was just too much. I didn't want to do it anymore. I was also rebelling against being smart.

Now, as I watch my oldest daughter go through the same thing, it hurts me because I remember this was how I used to be. The only difference is that she has me to push her and help her to understand that getting an education is something that she needs to do.

When Penn State came calling, I said to myself, *I'm not going to do it.*

Then, a major change happened. After my father was murdered, I received Social Security checks for support. Before my eighteenth birthday, the checks were in my mom's name.

Once I turned eighteen, the state sent the checks in my name. My mom said, "Hey, that's not your money. Cash the check and then you need to give it to me."

I said, "No."

She and I went back and forth about it. I decided that I was going to go to the check-cashing place, cash the check and give her some of it.

She was upset and said, "Now how am I supposed to pay my rent?"

I said, "I don't know. You have to figure it out." She insisted that I pay her rent, and I refused.

At that point, I told myself, *Well, I guess I can't live here.* I decided, *I've changed my mind. I'm going to go to college. I need to get out of here—and fast.*

That's when I went back to the Penn State recruiters and signed myself up, even though I knew I didn't want to do it. Going to Penn State felt like enlisting in the military. I also knew that attending college was the choice I had to make if I didn't want to keep putting up with my mom's nonsense. The only way someone in my circumstances could get out of where I lived was to go away to college. So, that's what I did.

I enrolled in college that day. It wasn't hard for me to get accepted since the Penn State recruiters made it clear that they wanted me. I went down to the recruiter's office, and I signed the paperwork. I prepared, did everything I needed to do, and then I went upstate away from Philly to college.

I went to college still hating school but knowing that

since I was on my own, I could do whatever I wanted to do. I told myself, *I don't have to listen to anybody.*

---

When I attended Penn State, I went to what they considered to be a branch campus, called the Berks Campus. I spent my first two years of college there. With the Equal Opportunity Program (E.O.P.), we took trips around the Tri-States. The people I met and became involved with were from similar areas or similar low-income families. I developed really close-knit friendships with many people in that program because we were always together.

During my first year of college, I played around. I decided, *I'm just going to show up because this is what they said I'm supposed to do.* I barely went to class. I only attended the classes that I felt like going to, and I only did the work I felt like doing. In the beginning, I had easy classes. The first semester, my classes were super easy, to the point where I didn't even need to go. I could just do the work and get straight As.

The next semester, when the easy classes changed into accounting, business management, and informational technology systems, it was hard.

During my second year of college, my grades started to show that I didn't really care.

Immediately, I shut down and I said, "You know what? I'm not going anymore. 'Cause I don't even know what they are talking about in this class! This class is boring. I don't want to be here."

I went from straight As to almost straight Fs. Then, I started getting these calls saying, "You're going to get put out of the E.O.P. program if you don't bring your grades up."

I was at risk of getting kicked out of the dorms because my GPA was too low. I started to realize, *Oh, no, these people are about to send me back home! Leaving home was the whole reason why I came here. Let me figure out how to get my stuff together.*

My E.O.P. coordinator, Mrs. Bruno, was a professor for one of my classes, and she took me under her wing. She said, "You can do this!" Every time she saw something that she knew would be great for me, she would make me aware of it.

I realized I wasn't going to get out of Berks Campus if I didn't raise my grades. I did get it together, so for my junior and senior year, I went to the Penn State main campus. It was in State College, Pennsylvania, but everyone called it Happy Valley. When I got there was when I realized, *Oh, this is totally different from what I'm used to.* I changed places from a small campus with a few thousand kids to a huge campus with over a hundred thousand students. Being six hours away from my family and friends was a big transition, and it was very hard. I decided, *I'm going to finish college, and I'm going to hurry up so I can get out of here and go back to what I'm used to, what I know.*

---

My first college degree is in hotel restaurant institutional management. In the beginning of my senior year, I landed an internship at the Marriott. At first, I was super excited because I figured they would want to hire me as a manager. They did hire me, but as a housekeeper. They told me, "You know, you need to work your way up."

I was not happy. I said, "Work my way up? I'm in college for this!"

I hated housekeeping—despised it. Before the new year had even started, I was no longer in that internship.

I learned that it didn't matter if I went to college and got a degree; that degree didn't guarantee me a job. That hurt when I realized I was suffering through four years in college for nothing. It's kind of like you did four years in jail, and then you get out and people are like, "Oh, you have a criminal background. So unfortunately we can't give you a job." Or, "We can give you a job, but we can't give you the job that matches your degree. We have to give you something that's beneath you. You have to work your way up."

I thought, *If I've got to work my way up from a housekeeper to a manager, then what did I go to college for? And it's not like I went to some fly-by-night school. I was at Penn State, a really good school.* I thought, *I don't wanna clean up after people.* Heck, I barely wanted to clean up after myself at that age.

During that time, I had an apartment and a roommate. My first roommate was really cool. I wound up living with one of my friends, Jackie, who was a year ahead of me. We had so much fun! Jackie was a trust fund baby whose father passed away and left her lots of money. And the girl had no clue what to do with all that money.

At this time, I believe I was suffering from bipolar disorder and manic depression. Every time I got stressed, I wanted to go shopping, which was a problem because I didn't have money like Jackie did. I messed up my credit score, obtained credit cards from everywhere, and bought stuff that I didn't need. Our two-bedroom apartment was filled with everything. If people needed something, they didn't go to Walmart, they would just come to our apartment.

Here's the funny part: we lived right across the street from Walmart. And we would not go to that Walmart. We would drive an hour and a half away in the middle of the night just to go to the 24-hour Walmart all the way across town.

We would leave our little town just to be able to say that we went somewhere. We drove all the way to Pittsburgh one time to go to the mall. Often, we had dinners and parties, and had all of our friends at our place. And it was just great.

And then, I got evicted. I remember being so upset. When I went to court, I tried to explain to the judge why I didn't pay my rent, but he just did not care. He said, "You've got ten days to get out."

And I said, "I'm about to graduate in a couple of months! I have to be here for class!"

This was in February, and my graduation was scheduled for May. Mind you, the campus was six hours away from my house in Philly. If I went home, there was no guarantee that I was going to be able to get back.

After I was evicted and was forced to go home, I found out about distance learning. At this time when I was offered the opportunity to go to school virtually, it wasn't as common to take classes this way as it is now. It took some time for Penn State to set up my classes. During that process, I had to explain to my professors why I was not physically in class. And that meant I had to tell all of my professors that I got evicted because I didn't pay my rent, which was humiliating. Most of my professors were pretty cool about my situation, however. They said, "I'll email you your work." Since the work I was doing for college mostly involved writing a bunch of papers, it wasn't too hard for me to complete my assignments from home.

I was able to finish out my classes that semester, which allowed me to graduate. I didn't attend my graduation ceremony, however. I felt embarrassed because everybody knew that I got evicted.

I didn't really want to go to college in the first place. Then, once I got there, I felt intense pressure to be the best because I always felt like I had to be perfect.

Even now, I'm always fighting myself mentally for that reason. It's something many people won't see, but that drive is in me. I'm always fighting, trying to work through my issues, and I would rather deal with them on my own.

What I learned about going to college is you get stuck with tons of loans and a worthless degree.

Why are my degrees worthless? At age eighteen, no one told me this; I didn't learn it until I was well over thirty. Here's an example:

Let's say 1/01/01 is the subject's eighteenth birthday, who we'll call Tracy. Tracy decides to skip college when she graduates from high school and decides to deliver food to people and sell stuff.

On the same day, 1/01/01, another young woman, Justine, turns eighteen. After high school, Justine goes to college to earn a bachelor's degree in business.

**1/01/01 Day One:**

- Tracy files for a Limited Liability Corporation (LLC)
- Tracy creates a one page website for the LLC and a business email, $5 a month business phone
- Tracy creates supplementary social media sites such as business Facebook, business LinkedIn, Twitter and Instagram.
- Tracy hires someone on Fiverr who takes about 2 days to create a logo for her LLC.

**01/02/01 Day Two**

- The Virginia Secretary of State approves Tracy's LLC.
- Tracy gets a Employment Identification Number or EIN

- Tracy applies for and gets a Dun & Bradstreet number
- Tracy inserts the Fiverr logo into the websites and social media channels
- Tracy applies for and gets a bank account with BREX and routes all her expenses and income through there.
- Tracy calls and applies for net accounts at Grainger, Uline, and Quill.
- Tracy gets one or two gas cards with Wex. She may have to give a deposit, she may not. Doesn't matter because she's spending that much money in gas monthly anyway.
- For the next month and a half, Tracy uses these accounts religiously, at least 3x for the invoices, until they report.

**03/01/01 Month Three**

- Tracy has a half-fundable Paydex score, and three months of business bank statements. Time to beef up the business credit profile with their proprietary system for a month or two.
- By the way, part of that beefing up process includes getting 2-3 $15k-30k business credit cards. Let's say her goal was $10,000.00. We'll round it off to $20,000.00 in limits to be safe. (Business limits are 10-100x personal limits. This $20,000.00 is considered a baby limit by the two banks in question.)
- Every major store has business accounts available, Tracy goes to apply for the correct ones at this step.
- Then she must wait three months.

**06/01/01 Month Six**

- At this point, Tracy's LLC has credit and six months of bank statements with a bank that reports debit card usage to the business credit bureaus
- Tracy now requests credit limit increases on the $20,000.00 of revolving credit her business has, easily doubling it to $40,000.00.
- Meanwhile, Justine is still in school learning about social psychology and her student loan debt is growing.
- Tracy has moved on to flipping homes and inventory at this point. She forgot about delivering food to people because it is no longer needed.
- Tracy's LLC is getting approved for some car loans, apartments and some business loans. Mind you, $10,000.00 is considered petty and Tracy's LLC now has a recommended credit limit (one of the scores the business bureaus gives) over $250,000.00. While she can't get approved for all because her business is under two years old, she's only eighteen, has a quarter of a million in credit limits, and is getting funded, paid, and solicited by American Express.
- Meanwhile Justine is still in school with ever growing student loans.
- Tracy will get denied for the first personal guarantee business loan application because she has no personal credit because Tracy never applied for anything. However she will get approved for the second one because she now has a credit profile.

What does this tell you? In just six months, you can make on being like Tracy and not like Justine.

**At the TWO YEAR MARK?!?!!?!?!?!**

- Justine is halfway through her bachelors degree and Tracy's business is buying a house. Not Tracy, but her business.
- Tracy then files for a DBA (doing business as) for her business that (in my opinion) says forget American colleges and universities because they're worthless. And this my friends is why I believe my degrees are worthless.

This is my experience and many other people's experience. In no way am I telling you to not go to college. I would just say pay attention and research everything first.

---

***"Have I not commanded you? Be strong and courageous. Do not be afraid; do not be discouraged, for the Lord your God will be with you wherever you go" (Joshua 1:9). I am curious by nature, this has helped me to understand myself by building confidence in my ability to be strong enough to go through all of the ups and downs that come with life.***

---

*Chapter Six*

# PROMISCUOUS PRINCESSES

***The number 6 represents the need to have a healthy balance between health, family, friends, and work.***

Every year a huge company would come to colleges and recruit students for an internship. During my sophomore year at Penn State, while I was still at the Berks campus, my teacher, Mrs. Bruno, recommended that I attend the "casting call" for the "Happiest Place on Earth."

That's how the internship came about. Ready for a change of scenery, I decided to apply for an internship/externship at the "Happiest Place on Earth" in Orlando, Florida. The recruiters talked about working for them, saying, "You want to be here! Imagine being able to put that on your resume."

I thought, *Yes, that's what I want. And I want to work at the Grandest Hotel. It's the most prestigious resort in the world.*

Every star who came to the "Happiest Place on Earth" stayed at the Grandest Hotel.

After the recruiters came to my school and interviewed me, I landed the job.

The first obstacle I faced was boarding on my first flight ever. Oh, my God, that was intense! I had never been on a plane before. I flew to Orlando, excited for a new change.

Once I got there, I hated it. I hated everything about it. First, the workers there were really fake. You had to get up and practice your smile in the mirror.

And we only made $6.15 an hour. We made so little, and yet we still had to pay rent. We didn't get to choose our living arrangements, either. I was assigned to share an apartment with three other strangers. My three roommates were...different. One was a complete nerd. Another was promiscuous. One was unbalanced.

The nerd roommate was always silent. I don't even know how she got her job because she didn't say anything! Her job was to be one of the characters, so she wore her costume in all of the intense Florida heat. Since she could have gotten overheated, somebody always had to walk her around. And now, looking back, I guess she landed the job because she didn't have to talk. In my opinion, I feel she had the best job of all of us.

The promiscuous roommate had sex with everybody. We even caught her in the act on the steps of our apartment! She wound up getting pregnant. I went with her to get an abortion because she didn't have anybody, and I didn't want her to go by herself. To keep her company, I went to the clinic and sat there with her. Her job was to be one of the princesses. She had a really good job because, for whatever reason, people like to get the princess jobs. Frankly, we all made the same amount of money, so I didn't know what the big deal was about it.

Then, there was the unbalanced one, the one I called crazy. Her job was to clean the park grounds. Even when she was transferred to work inside of one of the restaurants in the park, she was still the maintenance person.

One day, the crazy roommate and the promiscuous princess got into a heated argument. The crazy one had taken home some kind of cleaning solution from her job and sneakily poured it into the other girl's sweet tea. Being from Georgia, they make sweet tea all the time. Whatever she poured into her tea was a clear substance, so you couldn't tell by looking at it that it had been spiked.

When the princess tried to drink her tea, she said, "Something is wrong with this!"

I teasingly said, "Maybe she poisoned you. Maybe she put something in your tea."

She said, "Oh, no, can't be! Whatever!"

When we found out she really *did* put something in her drink, we were shocked. That's when we realized she was literally trying to kill us. To protect ourselves, we wound up kicking her out. And when she left, she had the nerve to take all of our groceries. The princess and I had to get groceries from the food bank

---

I first worked at the Grandest Hotel. It was the best hotel there and the reason I took the job in the first place, so I was excited. Celebrities like Nick Cannon, Justin Timberlake, and Michael Jackson would stay at the Grandest Hotel.

While I landed a spot at the Grandest Hotel, it was not for what I wanted to do. I was assigned to be a housekeeper, and as you already know, dear reader, I don't like being a housekeeper. To make it worse, as part of the housekeeping staff, I had to carry an umbrella and twirl it, and I had to wear a big old goofy maid dress while cleaning rooms.

Even though I was glad to be in the Grandest Hotel, I needed to get out of housekeeping. One day, I suffered from a seizure. After that, the hotel management felt housekeeping was not a good fit for me because I was working alone. And if I had a seizure again, nobody would know. Initially, I was glad to hang up my umbrella. However, after the seizure, I did not think too far ahead about where they would place me. I just was hoping they would put me in a different position that I could deal with.

Later, they switched me to a position as a hostess at one of their five-star restaurants inside of the Grandest Hotel. I said to myself, *Yes! I made it to the inside.*

My joy was short-lived, however. I was off to a bad start when my manager at the restaurant told me that she did not like my smile. Before my shift started as a hostess, she made me go into the bathroom and practice my smile. And I thought, *Lady, I don't have time for this.* If my smile was not to her liking, she made me go home that day. And if you went home, you didn't get paid.

As I stated earlier, we only made $6.15 an hour and we had to pay rent, and the majority of our paycheck went to our rent. As a result, I became stressed and wound up having another seizure. Right in the middle of dinner service, I passed out at the hostess desk. They called the ambulance, took me to the hospital, and gave me an IV.

Since I was at the Happiest Place on Earth under contract, if I left without a good reason before my term ended, I would be obligated to pay back a lot of money. That's when I decided to contact my doctor back in Philly. The doctor wrote me a letter saying I needed to quit because of health issues. A couple days later, management reached out to me and said,

"With your medical condition, unfortunately, we feel like this is not a good fit for you. We are going to let you go without obligation." Thankfully, instead of being there for nine to twelve months, I was there for about four months. I hated every minute of it.

When I hate something, I hate it with a passion, and I will change directions completely. I immediately think, *Oh, I have got to do something different. This is not going to work.*

That internship was horrible. I got to see the inside of a company that's supposed to be the happiest place on earth. But behind the scenes, we were not happy.

---

There are some moments in your life that are pivotal. If I had never traveled to Orlando for that internship, I would never have gone back to college. It was a really transformative time for me.

As bad as my internship experience was, it was yet another sign to me that it doesn't matter if you have a college degree. If you're coming straight out of college, companies are always going to give you entry-level positions. This realization inspired my thought process. I decided, *If I'm going to be in an entry-level position, I might as well skip going to college and just go directly into that entry-level position.* I thought, *What I can do is show off my skills. Then, maybe I'll move up the ladder versus going to college, spending hundreds of thousands of dollars in student loans, only to realize I'm still at square one.* While that moment was my realization about the pointlessness of college, as you will learn, I was naive because I went back and attended college four more times.

---

*"The LORD is my light and my salvation—whom shall I fear?" (Psalms 27:1). We need to accept that we may not always make the right decisions in life but we must also understand that failure is a part of our success.*

---

*Chapter Seven*

# REAL LOVE

***The number 7 represents a powerful source, a person's inner wisdom, intuition, and self-awareness.***

In September of 2006, I met my now-husband, Brandon. I walked into Bally Total Fitness for an interview. At the time, I worked at a nearby grocery chain but I wanted a part-time job. I selected Bally because I felt it would be easier if both jobs were fairly close to each other. So, I applied and was hired as the front desk receptionist.

Working at Bally was a pretty cool job; everyone was nice and I had fun with my coworkers. Brandon and I met and instantly became cool. We would talk, laugh, and joke. We remained friends for years to follow, and we shared a deep love for one another even though we stayed platonic.

I loved this man, and I knew he loved me, but I couldn't figure out why he wouldn't date me. I remember thinking, *Is he not attracted to me?* He would treat me better than the guys I was dating or talking to, but he never seemed really truly interested in dating me.

I was thirty-one when I realized that I was dating the wrong type of man. Actually, we had been best friends for about ten years at this point. When I moved to Virginia, he got married, and we stopped talking as much because his ex-wife felt threatened by me. We lost contact for a little bit.

Later, when he and his ex-wife divorced, Brandon found me on social media. At that time, I was living in Virginia. I helped him through his heartbreak, and he would come down to Virginia and visit me and my daughter. We would hang out and have fun, go shopping, and just do regular stuff together. After we started talking again, we both felt like we had never left each other. We still weren't romantically engaged or anything like that.

He later told me that he needed a change of scenery. And I said, “Why don't you just move down here?” And he did.

I believe right then was when we both realized we had been looking past each other and that we may have been soul mates.

Two months after he moved, we got together. I realized, *This is the person that I'm supposed to be with.* Soul mates we are. It was in the way that he treated me. I was used to dealing with guys who didn't have a job, who were “street pharmacists” or in and out of jail, aka “thugs.”

Everybody always told my husband and me, “You guys are made for each other.” We always said, “Nah, we're just friends. We're good.”

My husband was not my type physically because I liked tall, light-skinned guys. He was an average height, dark-skinned, bigger guy. However, I loved the way he treated me and how he cared for me and my daughter. I later found out I was not his type either. Finally, I thought, *I need to give this a try. Stop pushing him away.*

We had a conversation and he admitted he was doing the same thing! He said he kept thinking to himself, *I know I'm supposed to be with her, but I'm not ready for her yet.*

After we had a serious heart-to-heart talk, we realized that we were wasting time. We were supposed to be together. His one limitation was that he didn't want to cross a line and ruin our friendship. He was saying, "Our friendship is more important than taking this too far," and I finally said, "Forget it. Let's just see what happens."

Brandon and I have been inseparable ever since he moved to Virginia. We were thrilled when, even after many doctors said I couldn't have any more children, we conceived our baby girl. When we found out I was pregnant, we were ecstatic! It was music to our ears, so we decided to name our miracle baby Lyric.

We were trying to get our bearings between being together as a couple and as parents. Brandon went through a lot of ups and downs because he wasn't where I was mentally, physically, and emotionally. Since I was pregnant, my emotions were all over the place, but we managed to get through that. I felt that we were getting closer to taking the next step (marriage), so I began having conversations with Brandon about the things I would like and things I did not want or like when it came to getting married.

I told him that I didn't want to feel like the center of attention for my engagement. I didn't want it to be on a specific day like Valentine's Day or my birthday because I wanted to be able to celebrate those days on their own. So, he did exactly what I asked. He proposed to me in our living room. Since my kids were upstairs, he called them downstairs to join us. It was a normal, regular day.

On March 23, 2018, at around 10 p.m. in our living room,

with our children present, Brandon proposed to me and asked me to be his wife. I was excited, shocked, honored, and humbled as to how far we'd come. I was so grateful that he didn't put me on the spot in front of all of my friends and family. Actually, I wouldn't have minded a big reveal in front of my family and friends, but I know my husband would have been super nervous to propose in front of all those people. I told him I didn't want that so that he would feel more at ease. The poor guy was nervous as crap when it was just me and him (and the kids) there! He stuttered and hesitated, but it was great. It was one of the best moments of my life, and I will never forget it.

When we got married, it was on July 27, 2019. We chose this date because it was the anniversary of the day Lyric was conceived. If you haven't noticed yet, I'm really into numbers and how things make room where they want or need to be without your doing. God is good at doing things like this.

---

***"Love is patient, love is kind. It does not envy, it does not boast, it is not proud" (1 Corinthians 13:4). I believe that many of us fail in life because we aim too low. It is time we raise our standards.***

---

*Chapter Eight*

# "NO MATTER WHAT HAPPENS, MOMMY LOVES YOU"

***The number 8 represents success, material richness, and prosperity.***

While I was working on getting a bachelor's degree in healthcare administration, I lived in Rhode Island, and my mom was in Philadelphia. She had an aneurysm, had brain surgery, and then she got better. Then, my mom got sick again. Somewhere along the line, she wound up getting stomach cancer. I was her power of attorney, but since I lived in another state, I had to drive down to Philly every weekend. It was a six-hour trip both ways to check on my mom, talk with her nurse, and figure out what was going on with her health.

When they found my mom's cancer, it was stage four. Since it was in her stomach, the medical professionals felt they could cut out a large portion to get rid of it. They put her through chemo and radiation. I came to Philly to sign the paperwork before her surgery. The doctor discussed her options with Shamaine and me, because at that time, David was incarcerated. He told the two of us that if her cancer was to come back, there would be nothing else they could do for her because they would have taken so much of her stomach. That was January 17, 2009.

We decided to approve the doctors performing the surgery and to pray for the best. Mom had another stroke while she was under during the surgery. We could tell she was going down slowly. After the surgery, I made sure she was okay before I went back home to Rhode Island. After that, I would visit sporadically. This occurred during the time I was working online for my degree in healthcare management while working at the veteran's home in Rhode Island as a Certified Nursing Assistant (CNA).

On January 17, 2010, exactly one year later, we took my mom in for her one-year checkup. And the cancer had come back.

That's when the doctor told us, “It's bad. It's stage four again. There's nothing else that we can do.”

We asked how much time he thought she had left. He said no more than six months.

At that moment, I asked her, “Mom, what is it that you want to do?”

And she said, “Just don't let me die in the nursing home.”

I promised her I wouldn't.

I decided to move back to Philly so I could be with my mom and let her live out the rest of her days. When I moved back to Philly, I put my daughter in a daycare that was a couple doors down from my house.

The daycare personnel sent my daughter home one day with a soaking wet diaper that had leaked through her clothes. That showed me that they didn't change her. I was furious. I went to the daycare and I was going off on them, telling them what they had done. I didn't feel comfortable with my daughter returning, but I had to give them two weeks' notice. For those two weeks, she couldn't go to another daycare. That was the only reason I contacted her biological father and asked if he could come and watch her for the two weeks. I had just gotten this new job, and I was stuck. My CNA license hadn't been transferred back over to Pennsylvania yet, so I couldn't just go get a job as a CNA. I had to find whatever I could.

My daughter's father came over and watched my baby. However, he had other children with another girl. Apparently, she was a little salty about the fact that he had cheated on her and had a baby with me. I knew nothing about her until I was already pregnant. She would tell him certain things like, "I'm taking my kids away. You'll never see them again." He was stressed about this I guess.

One day, he took something. I don't know what he took exactly, but he was out of his mind, and he got upset.

My daughter was whining while he was talking to his girlfriend on the phone. She tried to make him feel bad about his decisions. He then decided to take his anger out on my baby and nearly beat her half to death.

I took my baby to the ER, only to find out that he stomped her. She was only two years old, and you could see his boot print on the X-rays and the CAT scans.

For whatever reason, the surgeon decided to blame me. The State Department of Human Services, DHS, took my daughter and would not allow me to be present with her. The surgeon called the police and the police came with guns drawn and arrested me.

While crying in handcuffs, I told my daughter, "No matter what happens, Mommy will always love you baby girl."

Meanwhile, my child's father was in the psych ward at another hospital for attempting to try to kill himself after he tried to kill my daughter. I had to get a lawyer to fight to get my daughter back. Meanwhile, I was still the acting power of attorney for my mom.

The Children's Hospital of Philadelphia and the University of Pennsylvania Hospital are right next door to each other. My daughter was in one hospital and my mom was in the other. I was going back and forth between these hospitals daily, making sure they were both okay. The only difference was that I couldn't see my daughter except for supervised visits because DHS had taken her.

However, I had an advantage. My ex-boyfriend's mom Towanda helped my siblings raise me since I was about twelve. She worked at the children's hospital for about twenty years. She talked to the social workers on the case and was somehow able to get me in so I could be there with my baby.

After my daughter was released from the hospital, the judge ruled that neither of our families who were blood-related could take my daughter, she would go into foster care. After hiring an attorney, the judge allowed my ex-boyfriend's mom Towanda to be the temporary custodial parent for my daughter since she was not blood-related. So, she took custody over my daughter, and then DHS allowed me to have supervised visits at Towanda's house.

On April 12, 2010, my mom came home to live with me. I fulfilled her request to spend her days at my house and not in a nursing home. It felt good to be able to honor her wishes. My daughter also came home the same day, as the custody order for her was restored to me. I was so happy and overjoyed that I threw a party for them with our family. We had a big cake and lots of food.

At the party, my mom wasn't her best, as she was in a

wheelchair. However, she was alert and talking, and everybody had an opportunity to see her. Barely a week later, she lost her ability to talk. Once that happened, I had to quit my job. I was living off of my student loan refund check because my mom's Social Security check barely covered anything.

From my experience as a CNA, I knew that she was dying. Since my mom's time was coming to a close, I began to reach out to family members and said, "If you want to see her, you might want to come down now." The exception was David because he was incarcerated.

I called the prison over the weekend and they let me speak to David. I said, "She's not talking. She's not speaking." I held the phone up to her ear and I let him talk to her. I said to her, "Mom, David's here. If you can hear him, blink your eyes." And she blinked.

He started to talk to her, then she began crying and he said, "Mom, I love you. It's okay. We'll be fine. I'm going to be okay. I'm going to be out of here soon. So, we are all going to be fine." She blinked again as if to say, "Okay."

Then, I called my sister Shamaine at work and told her, "Look, you need to leave work because it is happening."

Once she got there, she said, "Mom, fight the good fight. You can do this. Be strong,"

My sister got into an argument with her then-husband and told him to drop her and her kids off at my house. She woke up at four in the morning and went upstairs. Mom had shallow breathing.

Shamaine told Mom, "I see that this is hard for you. It's okay. We're going to be fine. If you need to go, it's okay." And then she said, "Mom, I'll be right back." She came into my room and said, "I think it's going to happen today. She's not looking good at all."

All weekend, and all through that night, I could not sleep

because I knew it was going to happen soon. I said, "Well, let me know when it happens. I'm going to try to take a nap."

Almost as soon as I had laid down, Shamaine came and said, "She's gone."

That was a day I will never forget: May 4, 2010. I think once Shamaine told Mom it would be okay, and once my mom heard that, she told herself, *Okay, I can go*.

I called the hospice people, the coroner, and then the funeral home. Mom's siblings came to see her, and thankfully, she looked peaceful. Throughout all of this commotion, I tried to hide what was happening with my Mom from my two-year-old, who had already had enough hardships for the year and possibly her entire life in my opinion.

It was hard to prepare and plan for the funeral. We had a lot of arguments because different family members didn't like the way that I was handling situations. But my mom had told me what she wanted, and I knew that I needed to make that happen, so that's what Shamaine and I did. Unfortunately, David wasn't able to attend her funeral because the prison wouldn't let him out.

---

The month of May is brutal. We had Mom's funeral the day before Mother's Day. And then the following week after Mother's Day is her birthday. Then the week after that is my birthday. May is no longer my favorite month. It's very hard for me.

So much happened in such a short period of time. I went through so many different emotions. I was suicidal. I was angry. At other points, I wanted everybody to pay, but for what? It was nobody's fault, but I wanted everybody to pay for it.

Now that I'm older, I realized God spared me from a lot of

things that year. I tried so hard to do some real-life damage to my daughter's father, and God just kept on sparing me, making sure that any demonic thoughts that I had were removed before I could hurt or harm anybody. Because when you think about it, that's your baby, right? If somebody harms your child—you are out for blood.

Over years of counseling, I have gotten to the point where I'm able to talk about this and not be angry, sad, or cry. It took me about twelve years. I was a different person back then. I've changed for the better now. I certainly watch people closely who are around my children, no matter who they are. I also watch who I allow to be around me and who I give my heart to.

During all the chaos and frustration, I was still able to focus on and obtain my degree. I'm strong-minded like that, but I don't know where that comes from. I can go through the hardest issues and the toughest things, and it will hurt me for some time, but once I put it out of my mind or realize it is a situation that is holding me back, I tend to let it go.

Resilience enabled me to go through that difficult time and also to have the strength to go through counseling and evaluate everything. When so much happens in such a short period of time, it's a lot to unpack. It can take years to unravel all the stuff that's been knotted up.

---

***"Do not be afraid or discouraged because of this vast army. For the battle is not yours, but God's" (2 Chronicles 20:15). God's mercy kept me so I wouldn't let go. Have you ever felt like just giving up? Say "God thank you for your grace and mercy that kept me". (Kurt Carr, "I Almost Let Go.")***

---

*Chapter Nine*

# BEING AN ENTREPRENEUR - NO COLLEGE DEGREE NEEDED - ENTREPRENEURIAL BLACK BELT

***The number 9 represents maturity, age, and knowledge. It emerges in your life when you have sufficient experience of life and are ready to take control of your destiny.***

I had a stroke in the teacher's lounge. At age thirty-two. And the crazy part was that I didn't even realize it.

Let me back up a bit. After I finished my degree at Penn State in hotel restaurant and institutional management, I went to the Art Institute of Philadelphia to become a chef. I had this ultimate plan in my mind that said, *If I'm going to own my own hotel or restaurant, I want to make sure that I know each and every part of it. So that way I'm never super stressed. If my cook calls in, I can just fill in for them.* I thought that I had all the answers to everything. I went to culinary arts school and received my degree in culinary arts. And then, I went to bartending school.

I didn't even like to cook or make drinks. Getting these degrees was purely strategic. It was in my nature to ensure that I had the right answers. The way I looked at it, I needed to become a chef because it had to match with my hospitality degree. And I needed to become a bartender, too, because the chef and the bartender are the two most important people in a restaurant. And if the chef and bartender called in sick to my future restaurant, we wouldn't be able to open. That wasn't going to happen on my watch.

During this time, I was infatuated with both Donald Trump and Gordon Ramsay. I admired the way they ran their businesses. My goal was to work at a prominent hotel or restaurant. I had the skills from my education and I had the drive. While I kept applying for lots of positions, I wasn't able to get a job as a manager.

Then, I got a job as a chef at a nursing home—I hated it. You couldn't make anything you wanted; it was just horrible. Cooking for the elderly and their dietary restrictions, I couldn't put salt in anything. I make the best Cream of Wheat, but when I cooked for our residents, I couldn't put sugar in it. I mean, the sugar lumps are the best part of Cream of Wheat! There was no challenge in it, either. It wasn't hard to put fruits in oatmeal. You didn't really have anything else to cook.

While I hated cooking at the nursing home, I fell in love with the residents. I would always sit and talk with them. Once I realized that I was really interested in helping the residents, one of the nurses reached out to me and said, "You have a really good vibe with these residents. Maybe you should think about coming to work on this side of the nursing home."

I said, "Okay," and I found out about becoming a certified nursing assistant or CNA. And then I went to school and became a CNA, and that was fun. I loved it.

I continued working at the nursing home as I loved all of our residents. Everything was good...and then, someone suggested, "Well, since you love it so much, you should become an LPN, a licensed practical nurse."

I decided to go to school for that. About 75% of my way through the LPN program, I found out I was pregnant with my oldest daughter. At that time, we were just starting our clinicals.

My teachers warned me, "Tiffany, you can't come to clinicals because you're five months pregnant, and this will be rough on you."

I fought them for a minute, and then we did a horrific wound care session. We had to treat a man who had a huge gaping wound in his butt. You could look into the wound and see so much, even his bones. If you've never seen anything like this before, trust me, you don't want to. The wound was infected. The smell was so bad.

I told my instructor, "Yeah, I'm gonna go ahead and head out."

By the time I had my daughter, if I had returned to the LPN program, my class would've graduated, and I would have had to start with a new class. I was not prepared to do that. But then something clicked in my brilliant mind. *You already have all these credits. Why don't you just go back to college and become a healthcare administrator? Then you could just run the entire nursing home.*

So I did that. I got a bachelor's degree in healthcare administration while I was still working as a CNA. I went to the administrator of my nursing home, and told him I wanted to shadow him to learn his position. I was happy when he allowed me to follow him, but I was shocked when he shared with me, "You're probably never going to get a job like this."

I asked, "Why?"

He said, "Because you don't have any experience."

I asked, "Well, how do I get the experience?"

He said, "You've got to figure that part out."

I said, "Oh, okay."

So then, once again, I went back to college, and I received a master's degree in business administration. You can't get better than that, right? It's an MBA...the creme de la creme!

I got a dual degree—a master's degree in business administration and a master's in human resources. With this degree, I'm thinking, *Boom, I am in there. There's no way they're not going to allow me the right to become a healthcare administrator now.*

And I was wrong.

"You don't have enough experience," that's all I kept hearing. "Enough experience, enough experience."

Through the craziness, I remember asking somebody, "How can I get the experience if nobody is willing to hire me?"

I decided to take matters into my own hands, because clearly I keep doing that. And I said to myself, *Self, I think that you should just go to school and become a teacher. That way, you can teach all those students what they need before they waste all their time, money, effort, and energy on school and loans.*

So...you guessed it. I went back to school. This time, I got a master's in education. In the Commonwealth of Virginia, you can't become a professor unless you have at least three years of K-12 teaching under your belt. I then began working on my degree to become a K-12 teacher.

While I was studying to become a teacher, I took a job working as a hospice CNA. On my first day on the job I met my now-best friend Brittney. Britt was my coworker but we clicked right from the beginning. She was five months pregnant with her youngest daughter. We talked everyday because we worked together but we spent just as much time together outside of work. Her family took me and my daughter in as their family. We would spend Thanksgiving and Christmas together. I remember I threw Brittney a baby shower at work and surprised her. She was shocked that I did that for her as we had only been friends for a few months at the time. We have grown to be best friends over the decade that we've known each other. Time flies but I eventually had another baby and Brittney is her godmother. Lyric loves Auntie BB and both of my girls love going over to her house. We were able to build a tight friendship because we had so much in common—not to mention we had both moved here from other states. We were inseparable then and we are still inseparable now.

After realizing that I wanted more once I received my final degree in education, I began to look for teaching jobs in my city. I was told I had to take and pass a test in order to become a teacher. I signed up for the test and took it a few different times.

At that point, I could not, for whatever reason, focus on passing the test for mathematics to become a math teacher. I kept failing the test by three points, and it was driving me crazy.

One of my friends said, "Well, you know, they hire teachers for special-ed, and you don't even need to pass that test right away."

I thought, *All right, cool. I'm gonna go and try that.*

I got a job at Henrico County Public Schools teaching special education for high school students. That was pretty cool. And then, I left that school because a lot of the people there were prejudiced. As a Black woman, I would walk down the halls and say, "Good morning, good morning," and the other teachers would just walk right past me like I didn't exist.

One of the teachers and I had to co-teach because we taught a class that was mixed with general ed and special ed.

The way it worked was that she was the history teacher and I was the special-ed teacher. I was supposed to be the backup who explained to the students who had special needs who might have an issue with understanding the assignment without my help. This teacher decided to tell her class that the people who live on the West End of Henrico are privileged and have money, and the people who live on the East End of Henrico are poor and they don't have internet or wifi.

So, one of my students asked me, "Ms. Lewis (my maiden name), you live on the East End. Do you have wifi?"

I said, "Yes, I do. And I have a vehicle."

My co-teacher was making it sound like people like me didn't have these things because we lived on one side of the Boulevard and another person lived on the other. I was thinking, *Lady, what are you talking about?* I decided, *Maybe it's not meant for me to be in the county; let me go to the city.*

I went to the city, and they paid me way more—but I found out really quickly why.

In the City of Richmond, I worked at an alternative school, where students who have a hard time adhering to the rules and regulations of regular school went. My time at that school was spent teaching the middle and high school students. The alternative school weighed heavily on me, and there was a lot of stress due to the students acting up. Therefore, I decided to apply to another school. Since the school was brand new, I figured this would be the best option. Boy, was I wrong again!

I wasn't there long because when I walked in, they had metal detectors. And that was enough for me; it was kind of scary even though I'm from Philadelphia. We had metal detectors in our high schools in Philly, but this was a middle school. So that made it even worse.

I continued to keep filling out applications for other

schools in the district until one opened up. I started working at Cary Elementary in Richmond.

My first principal was the she-devil. The other teachers and I rallied together and got her out of there after one year. No sooner had she left than we wound up with the he-devil. This was the she-devil's evil counterpart in my opinion.

I went through a lot at that school. I taught students in kindergarten through fifth grade, all of whom were special-ed and self-contained. "Self-contained" meant that the students were always under my supervision. Teachers and students went to the bathroom, lunch and gym together.

The principal threw every kid into my class. He must have thought, *This student can't read, so he needs to go to Ms. Lewis' class.* I had the bad kids, the special kids, autistic kids, the "everything" kids. The only thing I didn't have was help.

They decided to take my teacher's assistants (TAs) and give them to regular general education (gen-ed) teachers because they had thirty kids or more in their classes. They made me learn to navigate everything on my own. While I only had ten kids, I had to supervise ten special-needs kids every moment of the day, which felt like supervising fifty kids. When I complained to the principal and nothing was done by him, I went over his head and marched downtown to Richmond City Hall.

One day, I was sitting in the teacher's lounge, talking to my coworkers. And I guess somewhere in the midst of that, I stopped talking.

One of my coworkers looked at me with worry, and said, "Lewis, are you okay?"

I said, "Huh?"

Then, she said to me, "I don't feel good. I need you to walk me to the nurse."

While I walked with her to the nurse, for whatever reason, I kept rubbing my arm.

It never dawned on me when we walked into the nurse's office that my coworker was actually holding me up. It was in that moment that I realized that I was having a stroke.

That coworker saved my life, and the only reason why she even knew anything was going on with me was that nine months earlier, I was in a really bad car accident. When I was six months pregnant with my daughter, Lyric, a little sixteen-year-old girl, who was not paying attention, crashed into the back of me. She totaled my car and hers. Afterward, I kept having terrible headaches and bad migraines. I was relieved, however, when the doctors said my baby and I looked fine.

The accident happened in January 2016. Then, in March of 2016, on Girl Scout Sunday at our church, I could not handle the loud music from the band that was playing. From my previous medical issues with my seizures and asthma, I know my body. Whenever I feel like something is going on with me, I use an app on the back of my phone where I place my finger onto a reader and it gave me my heart rate and my blood pressure. That day at church when I wasn't feeling right, I put my finger on the back of the phone, and the app told me my heart rate was really high.

I thought to myself, *Okay, that's elevated. But I don't feel like my heart is jumping out of my chest or anything.* Still, I did not understand why my blood pressure was so high.

I talked to my husband (and this was before he was my husband) and said, "Hey, I need to go to the ER, something is wrong."

Since I was still pregnant, he was especially concerned. We left my oldest daughter with my girlfriend at church saying, "Look, we'll come and get her later."

We sat in the waiting room of the hospital for four hours with my head pounding. I finally got frustrated. I said, "Look, we're going to go to a different hospital because this isn't working."

We got up and went to a different hospital, where they brought me back immediately. They were concerned, seeing that I was pregnant, and noticed that I was having some kind of sensitivity to light. My head continued to hurt. Since I was pregnant, they couldn't administer their normal tests, like a CAT scan.

I'll never forget this one physician's assistant who kindly said, "Ms. Lewis, I'm very nervous that you may have an aneurysm, but we can't check as you're pregnant. Your baby is viable at this stage (meaning my baby would survive if they needed to do an emergency surgery)." At that time, I was eight months pregnant. She continued, "So, if something were to happen, we can get the baby out and save her. She would just be premature." She asked me to sign paperwork giving permission for the physicians to do this test even though I was pregnant.

I'm grateful that I signed the paperwork, and I hope that the physician's assistant is now a really great doctor because she went above and beyond to figure out the issue. She even told the physician in charge what she had found with the MRA and the CTA tests she performed, and he tried to brush it off, like, "Oh, no, I don't think that's it. It's probably the machine, the equipment here is old."

While the doctor tried to play it off, I saw something in the physician assistant's face. I thought, *She knows something. And she can't say anything because the doctor in charge probably told her not to.* I knew it had gotten worse when at 3:00 a.m., they put in an immediate transfer to take me to a new hospital. At this point, I still didn't know what was going on.

Even with the transfer ordered, the doctor was trying to make it sound like my issues weren't that big of a deal. He was saying stuff like, "Oh, our equipment is older here. So we're going to send you over to our sister location that does the neuro, blah, blah, blah."

My red flags went up even more when I went to the next hospital. As soon as I arrived, they already had a room for me and I had already been admitted. Mind you, when I was leaving the other hospital, they never said I was going to get admitted. I grew uneasy when they called in their X-ray and MRI team to come in to scan me in the early morning hours.

My room was right across from the nurses' station. I heard the nurse contact the surgeons and the neurosurgeons, saying, "Oh, we have a thirty-two-year-old woman and she's thirty-two weeks pregnant." And I heard her telling them, "You know, she has this carotid dissection."

I didn't know what a carotid dissection was, so I Googled it. That's when I learned what that wonderful physician's assistant had discovered. My right carotid artery had a dissection in it, which means it had a tear, and free-flowing blood was coursing through my system. And it was caused by the car accident. That meant I had this issue for two months and nobody knew.

Right after I Googled about the carotid dissection, I thought I was going to die. I could have died had they not found it and had I not gone to the doctor.

But the next morning, my obstetrician and the surgeons came in. They said, "We've looked at your tests. There's nothing we can do about it. You will have to stay like that for the rest of your life. There's a 90% chance that if we touch it, you're going to die anyway. So we might as well just let you do without."

Even to this day, I still have the dissection.

The first neurosurgeon was really harsh when he talked with me. My OB didn't like that. So the two of them had words back and forth. And then my OB confided in me, "I'm going to find you somebody else because I don't like the way he came off."

He did find a different neurosurgeon for me, who said the

same thing the first guy said, but he said it in a nicer way. I guess you could say his bedside manner was better. Now, every year in June, I get an MRI done on my neck and my head so we can make sure that the dissection is not progressing.

The blood is still free-flowing. It hasn't changed yet in all these years; it's staying like that. I take medication for the issue and the medical professionals tell me, "You don't have to worry about having a stroke. You're young. You're healthy." For some reason, at that moment I didn't feel reassured. I had high blood pressure and was pregnant.

The following month, I gave birth to Lyric. I had to have a c-section because they didn't want me to push, as it would cause too much strain on that vessel in my brain.

After the c-section, they continued telling me, "Okay, you're going to be fine. You're young, you're healthy. You won't have any issues, blah, blah, blah."

I went to see that doctor for the first time in June of 2016, and by September of 2016, I had a stroke.

---

Fast forward back to my coworker taking me to the nurse's office. When I had the stroke, my left side went completely numb. My hand was balled in a fist, and I couldn't get it to open. Normally, physicians give you Cortisone shots which release the muscles, but because of the carotid dissection, I wasn't like most people. They gave me the Cortisone, but they had to do that sparingly because they were afraid that it would make me stroke out.

After they gave me one shot, the doctor said, "Let's hope your hand opens up. We're only able to give you one more shot and then that's it."

So I just prayed. I asked God, "If it's meant for me to have this hand, it is Your will." In my teaching job, I had to do a lot of typing, which meant I needed to use both hands. But the left one wouldn't open. I went through physical therapy, and the therapist tried to get my hand to open up.

Then, I got the second Cortisone shot, and I was afraid because the first one had no effect—like, zero. But the second shot eventually loosened up my hand. It opened up, and now, it's as normal as can be. Thank God!

That was an incredibly difficult situation because I worked so hard to become a teacher. Even with all of my thousands of degrees, the fact that I was able to get a great paying job was astronomical for me. And then, in the blink of an eye, it was all taken away.

I had to be physically strong for my students. Even though it wasn't technically my job, sometimes I had to change their diapers and help them with their acts of daily living. They were supposed to have their own nurses or someone who did that for them. The he-devil would not bring those types of people in to help or assist me. If I couldn't lift my students, because some students in my class were in a wheelchair, I couldn't do my job.

My doctor put her foot down. She insisted, "It's not going to happen. I'm not going to sign off for you to go back in there to keep hurting yourself."

I refused, however. I signed an AMA (against medical advice) because I just wasn't ready to give up my teaching position. I worked so hard for this.

And then she made a statement to me that shook me to my core. She said, "What do you want more: to be alive to take care of your children or to die trying to take care of someone else's children?"

When my doctor shared that message, I had two reactions. First I thought, *Oh, she's not kidding.* Normally, she was friendly and often joked with me when I saw her. That day, she acted differently. She was stern.

"Do you really want to die taking care of someone else?"

She stopped me in my tracks. It made me think.

I just had a baby, so clearly, dear reader, you know what my answer was when my doctor said it like that. As much as I wanted to be a teacher, I knew I had to commit to being a mom first. That's what made me walk away from teaching and start my own career.

---

When I set my mind to do something, I put my whole self into it. In hindsight, when I look back on all the degrees I earned, I think I was trying to be accepted by my parents, my siblings, and my friends. I wanted people to know that I could do whatever I said I could do and whatever I put my mind to. And now, we've made it to my crossroads in life.

---

***"For God did not give us a spirit of fear but one of love and a sound mind" (2 Timothy 1:7). This is my favorite scripture because it aligns with my life. It helps me to understand that no matter what I go through God is right there with me so there is no need for me to be afraid. This is why I believe that I take those leaps of faith when some people may think I am crazy. Nope, not crazy, I just follow what God tells me to do.***

---

*Chapter Ten*

# YOU DON'T HAVE TO LIKE ME...I'M GOING TO BE ME REGARDLESS

***The significant meaning behind the number 10 means a higher purpose, higher self, inner peace, inner wisdom, and positive changes.***

I have always felt compelled to stand out from everyone else so people would notice me. After discovering my carotid dissection and having my stroke, I had to learn to mellow out a bit. I don't act like a chicken with my head cut off, running around doing all these different things anymore.

I was supposed to stay stress-free, too. We don't realize that, as we put more tension on our bodies, it goes directly to our brains. We're constantly thinking about stress; we're always worried about it. Stress will cause more blood to leak out of the hole in my carotid artery. That's what work was doing to me. My principal was stressing me out to the point where I just couldn't do it anymore. I couldn't take it. Even if I didn't have a carotid dissection, I probably still would have had that stroke.

---

After I spoke with my doctor and she gave me that new revelation, I allowed her to take me out of work as a teacher. I had a newborn baby, anyway, so I just stayed at home. I already had a couple of businesses that I would do on the side, so that is how I made my money.

For some time, I was an extreme couponer. I was one of those people who would go and get thousands and thousands of coupons. Then, I would go to stores and would purchase lots of items. I had yard sales every Saturday to sell the products I couponed. I was constantly adding to my stockpile, and then, I would go back to the stores and get more product and then do the yard sales all over again.

In addition, I helped college students with their homework. I tutored K-12 students, and at one point, I started a daycare in my home. I also did people's tax returns. That was how I made my money.

Those were my little side hustles. They wound up becoming really great hustles for a while after teaching. Eventually, couponing got oversaturated with so many people learning to coupon, and I got tired of fighting with the crowds for the items. I got tired of it and I just let it go.

After about eighteen years, I stopped helping the college students with their homework and that was not long ago. And I still do taxes. I've tried to stop, and my clients beg, "No, Tiffany, we need you. You can't quit."

The couponing, the yard sales, working with the students and taxes, everything that I've ever done in my life empowered me to help others. When I collect coupons and buy the items for next to nothing, then sell them to someone for less than what it costs them at the store, I'm helping them save money. And with tax returns, homework, and my work with my students, I'm helping. That's who I am, a helper.

I was born with an entrepreneurial spirit. I think that's why I kept going to school to try to be something different. I was scared that all these businesses, or what I would call "hustles" on the side, wouldn't sustain me. When I look back at them now as the business owner I am today, I really was an entrepreneur all along.

I was mistaken when I thought I needed to be working for someone else. I thought it made me feel comforted and safe because I knew I was going to get a paycheck. Being an entrepreneur, you don't know if you're going to get a paycheck, one day is great and the next day is not. For the entrepreneur, every day could potentially be a payday. It can be a rude awakening, though, because you might have made $5,000 yesterday and then zero money today. And then, you are looking at $20,000 worth of bills, so you hustle and try to doggy paddle your way back to the top of the water for a breath of fresh air. It can be frustrating. You have to come up with different ways to be able to brand yourself and to let people know that you do this type of work. It can be tiresome.

After my doctor gave me the ultimatum and I had to let my teaching role go, I didn't have a clear answer of what to do next. It made me nervous. I thought, *I'm going to choose my family because I think that's what I'm supposed to do, right?* Then, in my next thought, I would think, *Or I'm gonna feel selfish if I choose my career. Why do I have to choose? I have worked so hard for both. How do I choose?*

The biggest thing for me is that I'm really worried about what other people think. No matter how many times I say, "I don't care what people think," I really care. Someone else looking in on my life from the outside might judge me and say, "Look at her. She's selfish. She can't figure out which one to choose, family or career." Believing that people are thinking that makes me feel like other people are asking me to choose between my career and family.

I'm okay with people who don't like me, but I feel like they must have a valid reason why they don't like me. If you don't like me and you don't have a valid reason why you don't like me, I can't grasp it. It makes me think that something is wrong with me because I didn't do anything to you. Why don't you like me? The Gemini side of me reacts this way: once I gather that you don't like me and I grasp it, then I don't care what you think. At that point, it is what it is. It's easier now by not trying to constantly figure out why someone doesn't like me.

While I was dealing with these issues, I still had other obligations like I was the girl scout troop leader. Everyone in our troop depended on me to run the troop, sell the cookies, plan and book the trips, etc. I was overworked but I knew I needed some help. One of the new parents named Ruby decided she would step up and help me with the troop. Ruby was annoying but I saw something more in her. She was genuinely honest and caring. While everyone would constantly ask me why I'm friends with her. I would tell them y'all don't know her like I do. I began at that moment being very protective of her. I took her under my wing like a younger sister. She doesn't have any siblings as she's the only child but we are family now. I love Ruby and her children and vice versa. I'm very glad to have met Ruby and I'm glad we can raise our daughters together. We vacation together as a family and everything. I like being the older sister figure for Ruby because sometimes we need a sound board and we cannot always get that with everyone. So we help each other in different ways but it balances out our friendship and sisterhood.

---

When it came to my degrees, I felt torn because I had wasted so much time and money on getting all of my college degrees. At the time I left for Penn State, I needed to get away from my mom, and I felt my only options were to move in with my sister or go to college. So I chose college. I jokingly say that I'm going to call Sallie Mae, the nickname for the student loan company SLM, and tell her that she can come back and get all of these degrees that are collecting dust on my wall! I would think to myself and say, *Sallie, just forgive the 200 plus thousand dollars in student loan debt because I don't need those degrees. They're worthless, just a bunch of overly expensive pieces of paper.*

I'm not going to say that the degrees haven't done a lot for me, because they have. Since my degrees are based on business and ethics, my education has helped me to be more well-rounded in my business. Once I decided to create my own business, having a wide range of experiences prepared me for a number of situations. I still don't think that they were worth the amount of money that I paid for them, however.

In hindsight, even though I feel my college degrees are worthless, along with my side hustles and entrepreneurial spirit, they have structured my thoughts and built the strong foundation that I have now.

---

*"God is the same yesterday as He is today and forever" (Hebrews 13:8). I will trust you Lord. I need to know you're here. Through the tears and the pain, through the heartache and rain I'll trust you. So many painful thoughts travel through my mind and I wonder how I will make it through this time. Lord it's not easy, I will only trust you. (James Fortune, "I Will Trust You.")*

---

*Chapter Eleven*

# REALIZING MY WORTH

***The number 11 is considered a karmic number in numerology which means it is associated with a spiritual awakening.***

As I stated earlier, I met a boy when I was twelve years old. He had my mind mesmerized, and it made me feel good that someone noticed me and liked me at that age. We stayed in close contact for years. Both of our families were extremely close. I later met his mom, Towanda, and she was like the mother I never had. Towanda taught me so many things about life. She taught me about genuine love and affection. Before meeting Towanda, I had never experienced this type of love. It was very inviting and made me want to be around her always.

Because my ex was in and out of jail throughout our relationship, his mom and I grew closer and closer. Now, Towanda is my mom and no one can tell her or me anything different. Every major event that happened in my life,

Towanda was there. My proms, graduations, births of my children, my wedding, etc. Towanda has always been there for me, and I appreciate her for it. This woman has been through everything with me and I with her, so we will always be mom and daughter no matter what. Towanda is my mom, my kids' grandma and my husband's mother-in-law. If I didn't tell you otherwise I promise you would never know.

I moved to Virginia in October 2012, two years after my mom passed. My ex-boyfriend had been in and out of jail since we were around seventeen years old, but for whatever reason, he had this hold on my heart. He just couldn't stay out of trouble. When he got out of jail in December of 2011, we immediately got back together.

And then, in March of 2012, I found out that he was cheating on me and I left. I said, "I'm done. I don't want to be bothered anymore."

In April of 2012, after I graduated with my dual degree, a master's of business administration and a master's in human resources, I threw myself a huge graduation party cookout. And he crashed the party. His actions started a whole fight; he became angry because he thought I was with another guy. Really, it was just all friends and family at the party, but he blew up. Never had he put his hands on me before this particular day. At the party, he decided that he was going to punch me in my face. After he punched me I had a black eye, and it was the week before my graduation. This broke my heart. Because of his actions, I felt I never wanted to speak to him again.

Heading to my graduation, I drove eighteen hours to Clinton, Iowa. And the experience was horrible. I put makeup on for the first time ever because I had a black eye. Apparently, that graduation wasn't meant to be. It wound up getting canceled due to a tornado that blew away the entire outdoor setup. Later, I wondered why I had traveled there to begin with, because there was no graduation, and I received my degree in the mail anyway. So yes, it was pointless.

After that series of events, I decided, *I'm going to just focus on me*. I got a restraining order against my ex. I thought to myself, *I only moved back to Philly because of my mom. She's no longer here. Why am I staying here?* I decided I was going to move to Georgia. At the time, I started going to Georgia a couple of weekends a month.

I was ready to commit to moving when I found an apartment to rent. The day I was supposed to sign the lease and pick up the keys, I went on one last walk-through of the place and quickly told the management company, "Hey, this place is infested with fleas!"

They said, "Oh, my gosh, we're so sorry. We're not going to be able to rent it out. Blah, blah, blah."

I had already given my landlord in Philly a thirty day notice.

I had to move *somewhere*. Needing to make a quick decision, I thought of a really close friend I have, Jarina (we call her Buttons), who's more like my sister, who lived in Virginia. We grew up together and had been friends as long as I can remember because our mothers were friends. I came down to visit her with my daughter. While on that weekend visit, I decided that I would move to Virginia. I found an apartment, hired the truck, packed up all my stuff, and moved to Richmond. And I have been here ever since. That was October 2012 when I became a resident of the state of Virginia.

The experience with my ex was when I learned my worth. I don't need to be with somebody that will cheat on me, put their hands on me or my child. I never looked back!

---

*"The Lord is near to the brokenhearted and saves the crushed in spirit. This is who we are: the brokenhearted and crushed in spirit. And this is the truth, whether we are aware of it or not: The Lord is near us" (Psalms 34:18). There is no pain that Jesus can't feel and no hurt he cannot heal. All things work according to his perfect will. No matter what you are going through remember God is using you for the battle is not yours it's the Lord's. (Yolanda Adams, "The Battle is Not Yours.")*

---

*Chapter Twelve*

# BUILDING A BRAND!

***The number 12 represents good things that are on the way to those who are positively focused and trust in God.***

Once Brandon and I got engaged, I threw myself into planning our wedding. It was so exciting. I remember reaching out to somebody about creating our wedding invitations and was quoted 1200 bucks for 150 invitations. I was shocked. I told my fiancé, "For that amount, I'll figure out how to make them myself!"

I started researching and creating invitations. I learned about the machines, equipment, and process of making invitations. Since I'm a person with OCD, I bought everything. It took me a couple of months, but I made our invitations and save the date cards.

One of the machines I bought, the Cricut machine, is a vinyl cutter or a plotter. It can cut wood, vinyl, paper, cardstock, and other materials. My invitations were over the top and had an upward-facing envelope. It had a Tiffany blue tab you pulled, and the invitation appeared with all the information. The envelope had an imprint with our names, initials, and the date of our wedding. I had sparkly stuff down the bottom and the top, with a little bow with a diamond in the middle. It was extra and only a hundred bucks. I created 150 of them. I was so excited.

Later, I learned the same machines that I purchased to make the invitations can also make shirts. I reached out to Nakisha, a really good friend I used to coupon with. Nakisha lives in North Carolina, so we got on FaceTime. Over the phone, she taught me how to use the machine.

First, I made all of my bridesmaids' shirts. I was so excited that I posted it on my social media, saying, "Oh, my gosh, y'all look, I made this!" I didn't realize that so many people were watching me until they started asking, "Hey! Can you make this for me?"

As you know by now, I have a business mindset, so I thought, *Hey, let's turn this into a good old business*. This is where it all began—making t-shirts for my social media friends and family.

My husband gave me the name "custom" for my business since the designs are custom made, but spelled it with a K. We put a Z on the end to be different. And that's how the brand Kustom Kreationz was born.

Then, the hard work began.

When I started, I didn't even understand how Nakisha made the shirts. Nakisha made it seem so easy. I used to cry, saying, "Why do I have to do all of this?"

When you're working with vinyl, you tend to do a lot of weeding. Weeding is when you take a special tool and remove the extra material out from each design. It was tedious, and I hated it. I used to get so upset and say, "This is stupid. Why do we have to weed all this? What is the point? They need an easier way to do this."

That's how I got into a process called sublimation because I really hated weeding. Nakisha was my go-to person, and still is; I go to her for everything.

One day, I sent her a picture and asked her, "What is this? How do I make this? Because I have a customer asking me to make this."

And she replied, "Oh, you can't make that, that's sublimation."

I typed in "what is sublimation?" to text Nakisha, and then thought, *Never mind! I will figure it out.* I Googled and found a couple of videos on it.

Sublimation is a printing method that uses permanent dye ink instead of a plotter cutter (like the Cricut machine). The main difference between vinyl and sublimation is that vinyl lies on top of the fabric, whereas sublimation is pressed into the fibers of the fabric, so it lasts longer—forever, essentially!

And then in the next hour, I went and bought all the equipment I needed for sublimation. Within the two-week period of my initial conversation with Nakisha about sublimation, I was able to create the shirt for my customer.

When I sent the picture of my shirt to Nakisha, I said, "Oh, my gosh, I did it."

She said, "I know you didn't go out and buy all that stuff!" She was shocked. She explained, "I have the sublimation equipment sitting in my house, and I haven't even taken it out of the box. I've had it for over a year, and here you just went, bought it, learned, and did all this in like a couple of weeks!"

It took her about a year to learn about sublimation. The tables had turned, and I was able to repay her for teaching me about vinyl by teaching her about sublimation.

Then, Nakisha and I decided to start a group on Facebook, teaching people for free and showing them how to work with vinyl and sublimation. We wanted to share because everybody else involved in these creative tasks wanted to charge people.

With our free group, Nakisha and I allowed people to learn from us. In the first five months, we only had 250 people in the group. Then, I decided I was going to start asking other craft groups with more followers if they would allow me to post in their group, as long as it wasn't affecting what they were doing. A couple of people allowed me to share. One woman named Megan, in particular, went above and beyond and gave me permission to post my group link in her group of 15,000+ people. I gained over a thousand new followers overnight after posting in her group.

I made a decision. I realized that I didn't want to compete with everybody in my geographical area because it was really oversaturated with tons of people doing the same thing. Believe me when I tell you that there are hundreds, even thousands, of people who make shirts out of their homes and shops. That is when I realized the real money wasn't in making the shirts.

Here's an example: Let's say I make a shirt and then Mary sees my shirt. She knows how to make shirts, so she copies from my design. Mary sells her shirt for $5 less than what I'm selling mine for. And now, I can't make any money because everyone will go to Mary because she's cheaper.

The real money, I realized, was in becoming a supplier. If the craft stores shirts are $4 for one, and I sell mine for $2.50, you're going to come to me to buy your shirts. At least, that's what I thought. While I wasn't getting as big of a turnaround financially as the craft stores selling one shirt, I was attracting clientele because my shirts were cheaper than theirs. I decided to become a wholesale supplier.

One day, I realized I could really make a lot of money if I taught the people in my group how to do sublimation. At that time a couple of years ago, I decided, *Okay, if I teach them to do sublimation for free, then they will buy my products.* Nakisha and I purchased lots of blank items that you can sublimate on. After we did that, people started buying a lot from us!

I began my business in my office at home first. I had t-shirts, supplies, blanks, and all of my tools in a little space. It grew really quickly.

Once I outgrew my home office, my equipment expanded into our living room and into our kitchen. I had a heat press, a relatively small but very heavy piece of equipment, along with two desktop computers and a laptop. I started my business in April of 2018, and we moved in October 2020 to my storefront warehouse. So overall, I spent two and a half years working at home. If somebody were to walk into my house during that time, they would see organized chaos. And it was bad.

Initially, I placed the heat press on a folding table. Big mistake! It was so heavy that it started to bend and fold the table. It also had a huge cord, which was a big tripping hazard. I kept tripping the circuit breaker, too.

One night, there was an electrical fire. Fire started crawling up the wall of our house! It was 8 p.m., and I had to call an electrician for an emergency fix, which was expensive. By the time he fixed the issue at midnight, I had to complete a bunch of orders, causing me to stay up until 5 a.m.

In June 2020, I finally incorporated my business. I decided that it was time because I realized I was moving in a new direction. The number of wholesale items and blanks coming in had increased to a point where I needed help. At first, I tried to bribe my oldest daughter into helping me. She wasn't too keen on it, so I hired my first employee. After interviewing students who were interested in crafts, I hired a high school student. When she became overwhelmed, she brought in her mom to help. And then, when the student returned to school, I hired her mom.

During the global COVID pandemic, which started in 2020, we added the student and her mom as part of our "pandemic bubble," which meant they were allowed in our house, along with me, my husband, and my kids. Anyone outside of our bubble, including clients and vendors, had to pick up or drop off products on our porch. Sometimes, we placed items in our mailbox or shipped them. Whatever was thrown at us, I found a way to work around it.

I decided with the growing success that I would try to expand by starting my own sublimation paper line. With two employees and myself working out of my living room, it was time to find a new home.

In August of 2020, I realized that I needed to find a space for Kustom Kreationz Wholesale. I had ordered several pallets of paper, and I had no place left to store them at home. It was time to take care of business and find a new business location.

---

***"Commit thy works unto the LORD, and thy thoughts shall be established." (Proverbs 16:3). When you create a business idea and plan and share it with God, He can make sure that you accomplish it. There's nothing like inviting God to be a part of your business.***

---

*Chapter Thirteen*

# TAKING CARE OF BUSINESS

***The number 13 is often considered unlucky by those who are superstitious, but 13 is very auspicious.***

I started Kustom Kreationz LLC in 2018 from my house. When I got engaged that year, I probably made about $10,000 off of this business, which felt like next to nothing. I was working so hard, yet I felt like I was making a million shirts. I realized that I had to do something different. In January 2020, I started a Facebook group, K&T Kustom Crafts and Sublimation Blanks Hosted by Kustom Kreationz, and initially, we didn't have a lot of followers. We were spending a bunch of money buying all the items, but nobody was really buying supplies from us.

It took about six months for the group to grow. I met and became friends with another crafter in my business, and she allowed me to post my Facebook group links in her group.

Her group had 15-20k people in it. And then, I gained a thousand followers overnight. Within the next week, I had thousands of followers thanks to Megan. Now that we had thousands of paying customers, we were swamped with orders.

Maybe two days after that, I knew I needed a business bank account. I needed it because my PayPal account went from making a thousand dollars a month to $3000 in one day.

I incorporated the business, I opened up a business bank account, and created a website. Taking these steps were the best things that I could have ever done. My website launched on October 1, 2020, during the middle of a global pandemic. By December 2020, I finished the year with almost a hundred thousand dollars in sales in about two months. I said to myself, *Oh, wow, this is crazy.* It didn't matter to me that I made a hundred thousand because I used that money to reinvest and replenish everything that I sold. And then, in 2021, I started carrying my line of ink. I released four new products in 2021 alone.

Since I spent a lot of the money that I made in 2020 on those products, in 2021, I was able to reap the benefits of selling those products. During that year, I looked at my profit and loss statement. And I realized that I had made over $500k in my first full year as a wholesaler.

Even with success, I'm torn. A part of me thinks, *This is awesome! Look at what I've done.* Another part of me gets sad when I look at my profit and loss statement. Even though I have grossed a lot of money I have spent a lot of money, too. My goal now is to be at the point where I'm able to say, "My business pays me."

When people learn how much I've grossed, I'm really quick to share, "I'm not making that amount of money. My business is." I tell people this because it is one thing for your business to gross an amount, but it is another thing to see how much money you've netted. For example, if my business made $500k, it may have netted $50k after paying for supplies, products, payroll, rent and other utilities. Unless you run a business and understand how it works, you'll never get it. For that reason, I try to educate people about business credit.

When I posted about my new business credit card on social media, people began inboxing me asking, "Wow, why do you go and apply for all these credit cards? Aren't you afraid you're going to owe all this money or go bankrupt?"

I tell them, "If you get a credit card, just because they give you a million dollars, doesn't mean you need to spend a million dollars!" It's the teacher in me. I tell them, "That's the reason why I'm trying to educate you guys."

I want to teach everybody or anybody who wants to learn about business credit, because it is wiser to leverage someone else's money than to use your personal money.

At this time, I was still learning about business credit. I applied for a bunch of business credit cards, and they sent them to me in the amount I requested. American Express gave me an Amazon credit card, and it was only for $3,000. So I thought, *Oh, gosh, I don't want to be bothered with them.*

Then, I applied for another American Express card, and they gave me a limit of $80k. Days later, I applied for yet another American Express, and they gave me a Plum card for business. I called and asked American Express, "What is the spending limit?"

I spoke to a representative who said, "Oh, that card doesn't have a spending limit."

I asked, "How does that work?"

He said, "Well, whatever you want to purchase, you just call in and you tell them, 'I want to purchase this.' And then they give you the okay. And then you swipe the card."

I had to try it out, and said to myself, *Let me see if I can use this card without me calling them.* ' I spent $46, swiped the Plum card, and it said "approved," just like any other American Express business card.

Later, I got a call from this random man on my business phone, which was strange because I never answered my business phone.

He said, "My name is John. I'm calling from American Express."

I was thinking, *Oh, Lord. They caught me.* I cleared my mind and said, "Yes, how can I help you?"

He said, "I'm calling to offer you a line of credit for your business. A line of credit is cash flow. Do you need cash flow for your business?"

"Yes, of course, who doesn't?"

"Okay, just send me this information. And then I will see what I can do with the underwriting team," he replied.

I sent him my bank statements for the last few months.

He said, "Wow, this is impressive. What do you do?"

When I started telling him, he said, "You're making all this money making shirts?"

I said, "Not exactly. We have a wholesale side to it."

After I explained to him what I did and how I decided to be a supplier, he said, "Wow, that's awesome. And how long have you had the business?"

I said, "Three years, but I just incorporated it last year."

"Really? So between this year and last year, how much did you make?" he asked.

"Well, last year I was at like $240k, and this year I made $520k so far," I said.

He was blown away and said, "I'm pretty sure I can get you approved."

I said, "Okay, that sounds great."

Right before I had this conversation with him, I had

applied for a Wells Fargo line of credit, but they denied me, so I didn't really expect anything. However, I did get an email back from him a few hours later, saying, "Congratulations, you've been approved for a $150k line of credit."

I said, "Great. Let's do this."

Even though I was happy to be approved, the truth is that I had nothing that I needed to buy for my business at that time. I reinvested all the money I made the previous year on restocking merchandise. But the fact that I have the credit line now is great if I ever need it.

The gentleman from the credit card company was really nice. He explained to me how to get higher lines of credit on the card. He encouraged me to use all the money. And he said, "I don't care if you take any bill you have and use the credit card to pay it because you're going to have to pay those bills anyway. So take it, use the credit card or swipe it, pay all your bills, then take that money that you were going to use to pay the bills, and then pay the credit card back. Once they see you using the credit limit, they will increase it without you even asking."

I purchased a gorgeous new bedroom set in midnight blue with the card and paid it off in full.

I try to explain this information about credit cards and other info I've learned while in business, but people just don't listen. They don't understand the building of the business credit. It's really simple. If you don't use it, you will lose it.

While I am no longer a teacher in a classroom, I still am and will always be a teacher at heart. I have a masterclass that I added to my website, a four-hour course, that teaches business one-on-one. I started with teaching how to get your Employer Identification Number (EIN), obtain your Dun & Bradstreet (DUNS) number, incorporate your business with your state corporation, and check your business name to make sure nobody else has the same name. I love teaching people how to brand their businesses, grow their businesses, and fund their businesses.

Too many people think making shirts is easy and quick money. But once they buy the equipment, they realize it's not that easy. They definitely will have to work extremely hard in order to make a million dollars even though it can happen!

There is a young man from Philly who went on *Shark Tank* selling his clothing line, and he's a self-made millionaire. But people need to learn the steps to take to get from making clothing to making money from their products.

That's why I'm trying so hard to get on the television show *Shark Tank*. Hopefully, one of the sharks will become my business partner.

People often ask which shark on *Shark Tank* is my favorite. My answer is all of them, including the guest sharks.

If I were to get a deal with Mark Cuban, I would consider this a great deal because I would have the opportunity to make items for his basketball team. If I got a deal with Damon, that would be awesome because he's the founder of the clothing line, FUBU, which is extraordinary. He would make my business go to an extreme platform. If I got a deal with Barbara, my products would go on the shelves of every Bed, Bath and Beyond, Michael's, online websites, and in shopping malls, everywhere. If I went in with Lori, I would be on HSN every other day with sublimation printers and supplies. With Kevin, aka Mr. Wonderful, he'd have to give me a really good deal because he likes to take a lot of equity or add royalties. Kevin is brilliant. No matter what, he would raise the stakes of my business to the maximum. I like Robert because he's so passionate. I feel like he would put my business on a different platform. I really would love to do a deal with the Spanx founder, Sara Blakely. I don't know how we would link up or how we would do it, but I just love her goals, her mindset, and the way she makes money.

***

When it comes to business, I like to say, "If I see a problem, I'm going to solve it. You know what? I'm not just going to solve it, I'm going to make the solution even better." Even in this business of making shirts, I'm still helping people because I'm teaching them how to start their own businesses. I think everything that I've ever done is centered around helping others.

---

***"Happy is the man who finds wisdom, and the man who gains understanding" Proverbs 3:13). You need to be a lifelong learner in order to be successful in business. You should constantly seek to improve yourself and increase your knowledge about running a business.***

---

*Chapter Fourteen*

# GROWING SUCCESS

***The number 14 is a unique number that is normally associated with knowledge, travel, and exploration of unknown territory. This number gives a person the ability to learn, study, and grow.***

With growing success, I decided, *You know what, I'm going to start my own sublimation paper line. Yep! That's what I'm going to do. And then all the people I'm teaching to do sublimation for free will buy my paper and make my brand more popular.*

I'm a thinker. Once I have an idea, I think it through immediately right then and there, and I just go with it. So, I jumped into action.

I purchased the paper, starting with a sample. I spoke vigorously with the vendor in China, explaining to her what I wanted. I described everything I wanted in order to save time and help my sublimation community. I showed all of the samples I purchased to my group. They immediately asked for pre-orders.

I had over a hundred pre-orders for packs of paper, and they weren't even manufactured yet. In October of 2020, my first shipment of paper came. I was super excited. By January of 2021, I started my sublimation ink line. Before I began my line, the only person who had good ink at that time was a guy in Atlanta. He was awesome, but he was always sold out.

Meanwhile, my group grew to 2,000, 3,000, and then 4,000 people. And they were all complaining, "This ink is sold out! What kind of ink can I use?"

I saw their need and said, "Okay, I'm listening to y'all." That's when I decided to make Kustom Kreationz a one-stop shop and a household brand name.

Before I offered my products, customers would have to buy supplies from China where they're made. There are some places in the U.S. that sell sublimation inks and other items, such as Amazon. The problem with Amazon, though, is that vendors claim to sell sublimation products but they aren't the right products. People will buy them, end up getting the wrong supplies, and then realize the items don't work. Your best option is to find somebody who is local and who has a following and a website that's legit. At the very least, a supplier needs to go live on social media so people know that they are a real person and not a robot.

At the time of writing this book, I am figuring out how to get into Walmart stores. While my paper does sell on Amazon and Walmart.com, I want to get it into Walmart stores, Michael's, and other craft stores. Surprisingly, craft stores don't sell any sublimation supplies—no ink, no paper, nothing. I have a vision that my whole line could be carried in those stores, and everybody would make so much money. From my customers to the businesses my products are sold in. I need a way in because I know I will become a multi-millionaire or even a billionaire.

When I first started reaching out to vendors in China, it was both hard and easy. When I told Nakisha that I was thinking about starting my own sublimation paper line, I asked her, "How would I go about it? "

And she told me to just go on Alibaba, which is like Amazon but located in China. I used a Chinese website and did some research. I already had vendors I worked with for my sublimation blanks that I was selling. I went back to my current vendors and asked if they made sublimation paper. And when they said yes, I asked them to send me samples. When I found the right sample, I asked the vendor to tweak it the way I wanted it.

The biggest challenge when I started doing sublimation was the number of steps involved. You had to lint roll the shirt. You had to line the shirt with parchment paper in the middle or else the ink would go through to the back. You had to tape the sublimation paper onto the shirt with heat tape. You had to put another piece of parchment paper on top of the shirt. You had to put butcher paper underneath the shirt. The number of different steps you needed to take to make a shirt was overwhelming.

I thought, *I don't want to do any of these steps anymore. I want to develop a process that will allow you to just print and press. Nothing more, nothing less.*

So that's what I created.

Now, with the improvements I requested, the shirt is pressed in sixty seconds. I bought my ink from the same vendor from whom I purchased my paper. The vendor paired the ink and paper together so that they become a perfect match when they are pressed.

The next item I added to my product line was sublimation shirts. Most polyester shirts on the market are made with jersey material, which feels silky and slinky. I didn't want my polyester shirts to feel or look like that. I wanted them to have a soft feel—like cotton. I was really particular about what I wanted. I was determined to create the perfect shirt.

I learned about GSMs, or grams per square meter. This is similar to thread counts for quality bed sheets. I wanted fabric to have a certain number of GSMs, which would make the shirts softer and have a more cottony feel. After the vendor and I discussed the GSMs, I decided to purchase a few samples of the shirts to see the quality for myself. Once I received the samples, I was in love! I immediately decided to press something on the shirt to see how my paper and ink aligned with these particular shirts. I was impressed that the vendor did exactly what I asked. I did not need to put any paper down. All I did was put the shirt on the press, place the printed image on top, and press it.

Once I did that, it was definitely a game-changer. I knew from that point on that the shirts with my ink and my paper were going to blow up in the market! And they did.

It wasn't an easy process getting to that point. The vendors speak English, but if you say something to them that they don't understand, then you have to find another way to explain things. While they know about GSMs, there were still language barriers for both parties. Initially, I didn't know that there were certain HTC (Harmonized Tariff Codes) that I needed in order for the U.S. to allow my products into the country. The vendors were putting the wrong codes on my items, and because of this, my products were getting stopped at the border. I had to get a U.S. agent to work around it.

I went through two or three different agents in the U.S. because they were expensive. Now, I've learned you really have to educate yourself in your business *and* their business, because otherwise, you will burn a lot of money, time, and energy. Now, I know a lot more about business, including information about the codes and the GSMs I want for my products, etc.

For my line of supplies, I launched my paper first, then ink, and then the shirts. I was very proud of my product line and the direction in which it was going. All of my products sell really well. But the shirts are the star of the line. Eventually, I realized that people grew tired of the fact that you can only sublimate on white or light colors. I came out with my brand of OBM Sublitextile fabric (Easy Sublitextile) that you can press onto cotton, jeans, or any kind of fabric easily. Easy Sublitextile is a product that allows you to sublimate on materials or fabrics that you normally wouldn't be able to sublimate on. This allowed my customers to expand their businesses without limitations. With all of the items in my line, my business has been going up.

---

***Observe what the LORD your God requires: Walk in obedience to him, and keep his decrees and commands, his laws and regulations, as written in the Law of Moses. Do this so that you may prosper in all you do and wherever you go. (1 Kings 2:3) This entire book shows that I am one to step out on faith without any other information. I love that about me but sometimes it can be a gift and a curse. Either way I know with God on my side I WILL NOT FAIL!***

---

*Chapter Fifteen*

# TO BUSINESS HELL AND BACK

***The number 15 is referred to as the manifestation of a harmonious life, a synthesis of matter and spirit.***

When I Googled my business name Kustom Kreationz, a bunch of other businesses appeared. I didn't know I had to get a trademark for my business until I did that search. I started to do more research. First, I learned about my DUNS number, which stands for Dun & Bradstreet. This is a unique identifier number for businesses and was the first step to getting my trademark. I found out once I received a trademark, I could trademark the name of my business and my logo, which means nobody else would be able to use them federally.

Initially, I paid a company that was supposed to apply for a trademark on my behalf. They clearly didn't do a good job, however, because the US Patent Attorney's Office (USPTO) contacted me and let me know my application wasn't filled out correctly. I fixed it and sent it back. The next thing I know, I get another call from the USPTO, saying, "You're going to have to redo this. We can't give you this name because it's too popular."

I told their rep, "I already have products with this name on them and with this logo. And these products are already selling."

She still said, "No, I can't give it to you."

I waited nine months to receive a denial letter. Then, I found an attorney who deals with trademarks and contacted them about my situation. After they charged me the attorney fees, I had to pay the trademark fees again. After they received the fees, it took another ten months to get the trademark approved.

Once I received the approval, I was feeling relieved the process was over. However, the USPTO contacted me and said, "We just realized you carry paper, ink and shirts. You need a trademark for each."

That's when I learned my trademark only covered the sublimation paper. I decided not to trademark the shirts at that time. I would've had to pay more money because the shirts are in a different category of products. Then, I added the ink to the trademark, and they charged me an extra $600 for that.

I wound up paying thousands of dollars to get the trademark, and it took over eighteen months to get it. Since it was such a difficult process, I was a prime candidate to get scammed by a company.

When you get a trademark, you go onto the Uniform Commercial Code (UCC) Filing List. Recently, a company reached out to me and said that I was under investigation because of my UCC filing. This company then told me that they are attorneys and they could fight for me to keep my UCC filing in good standing. They said, "We see that you have an MCA (Merchant Cash Advance), and we can help you by negotiating with the company you got the loan from. The money will go into an escrow account and then we'll pay them to settle with them on your behalf."

I thought, *Okay, cool.*

I researched that company and it had great reviews so I signed a contract and I let them go into my bank account and take the money out. It wasn't until three weeks later that I started realizing something was off because the other company kept calling me about my loan. I thought, *If this company has done this work on my behalf, why is this other company calling me?* I researched the company again that was supposed to help me fix my current issues only to find out that company was a fraud and scammed me. They even made up their own reviews. They took a lot of money out of my bank account, causing me to default on my loan. This also caused the loan companies to try to sue my business. I asked the bank to go in and investigate that company. As of the time of writing this book, the bank is in the process of investigating them now.

The crazy part is while I was going through this situation with my bank, I found out that I got scammed by another company. And I didn't even know it.

I paid a company to promote my marketing for my business, including my website and social media ads. I was paying them almost $2,000 a month and I didn't even make $1. I reached out to Facebook and asked, "Is there somebody that can help me with this? I must be doing something wrong because I am getting no return for my marketing."

One of their employees called me and said that to have an impact with marketing on Facebook should only take a few dollars. She sounded surprised and said, "It shouldn't cost hundreds or thousands of dollars."

And I said, "Well, it is."

After she looked, she saw the marketing company had only spent $7 on marketing, and that was months earlier.

I then spoke to the bank and they said they saw a charge for $500 from the marketing company. The bank rep asked, "Who did all this money go to?"

I said, "I don't know. I didn't even know that the money was missing."

Getting scammed by companies hinders my decisions and impacts what I'm thinking and what I'm feeling. When you lose trust in other companies, it is an issue. You have to keep working and keep moving, however.

---

The biggest issue that I've had being a business owner, entrepreneur, and a boss is the constant loss of employees. In my first year, I went through six employees. It was horrible. Some got fired, some quit, and some were no-shows. Some got fired because they were messing up. Some got fired because they weren't doing enough.

I take time to train everybody myself. When I train you directly, I know that you know the process. I don't have patience for you to say that you know how to do something, and then you still mess up anyway. If you pay attention to what I tell you, it's not hard, and you'll do great.

Another big issue that I have with my business is the amount of money I have made and lost for different reasons. Sometimes with shipping, the products are packaged incorrectly, causing them to be damaged when the customer receives it. There have been plenty of times when the sublimation ink has leaked all over the box.

Another big headache has been getting a U.S. agent that is reliable, resourceful, and has integrity. My vendor in China sent me a U.S. agent's info; the agent would pick up my products and bring them to me once they made it to the United States. The first company that they sent me to, the staff could barely speak English. Due to the language barrier, I never used them again.

So I asked my vendor to help because I was so irritated that I couldn't really understand what they were saying. I felt like that company was charging me more than what it should have cost.

I said, "I need a U.S. agent who speaks English in the United States who can handle this for me."

She connected me with a Black-owned agent, and in the beginning, everything was great. I wasn't paying much for shipping, and the first and second shipments went smoothly. By the time I got my third shipment, however, I went from paying next to nothing to tens of thousands of dollars for one shipment—about $20,000 to ship the items from New York to Virginia. I wound up taking out merchant cash advances because I couldn't afford to come up with $20,000 or $30,000 in the blink of an eye. If I didn't get the products and I left them at the shipping location, the United States would've put them into storage and charged upwards of $200 per day. When all of this occurred, I was in Costa Rica on my anniversary trip.

I had no choice but to take out the merchant cash advance. When I returned from my trip, I began doing some digging—I can be like the FBI when I want to be. If I get too fed up and can't figure out why something happened, I dig and dig until I figure it out.

I talked to plenty of shippers, and I even talked to the

people who delivered the products, and they showed me how much they normally charge to deliver. Since they were only charging a few hundred or a few thousand dollars, I had to ask why my U.S. agent was charging me tens of thousands of dollars. I figured out that my U.S. agent was charging me more and then pocketing the extra amount for herself. That's why I fired them. Technically as of the writing of this book, I have no US agent. It's frustrating because I'm ready to import more items.

---

The biggest decision that I have made in this business thus far, in my opinion, was the decision to stop selling blanks. Selling blanks is how I began my business. On the wholesale side, blanks are the items that you sublimate on. They range from cups, mugs, tumblers, shirts, socks, backpacks, pocketbooks, and more.

I started to realize that vendors from China, who were normally the third party or the middle-man decided that they didn't want to be the middle-man anymore. They came to our platforms, where we market our products, and then began to sell to our customers. And when I say they were undercutting us that's an understatement.

When I first started working with vendors in China, you needed to have a MOQ, which is a minimum order quantity. Currently, the vendors don't even care if you have an MOQ. They just want your money. If you are an entrepreneur like me who sold wholesale blanks, those products started just collecting dust because most people now know that they can go directly to China and purchase blanks. And it's going to be cheaper because it's coming directly from the manufacturer.

I realized in the fall of 2021 that I needed to let go of the blanks because the pricing issue was just going to get worse.

I was definitely right, because now, the Chinese vendors are selling the stuff themselves. It was tough, but I decided to do a three-month, 50% off sale on my blanks to get them out of my warehouse.

I made that call even though that was a hard decision for me to make, and I knew it was going to make my business take a crazy downturn. I knew it would be better to get the products out and make the money that I could make off of the blanks before they were worthless. So, that's what I did. And once I did that, my sales immediately tanked.

In the first half of 2021, I made $660,00. That's about $330,000 per quarter. For the first three months of 2022, I am currently at less than $20,000 for the quarter. So, as you can see, the drastic drop in revenue caused me to make some drastic changes for the business.

I decided to do a crowdfunding campaign for my business on GoFundMe to help with upcoming purchase orders. I'm working really hard and pushing myself and the business to make it better and to teach more people. But that also weighs on me;  I don't have a lot of time to spend with my family and my children. So this is why I thought crowdfunding would be a great option but I was wrong again.

It's stressful. Every day, I was trying to figure out a new way to make money. That's not a way you want to live or run your business. And when people don't understand that and make assumptions about what they believe or they feel, that's hard to deal with and causes unnecessary stress and anxiety. People took it upon themselves to assume that I didn't need the crowdfunding and bashed me for trying to do it. I eventually said forget it I'll figure it out myself. When people try to back me into a corner I tend to get out and get far away from those types of people.

Even though you are deep in the valley, there are still mountains to climb. Once you have overcome the deep valleys and the tall mountains, you will be able to soar to your highest potential.

Know this, if you are going through hell right now, it will not last forever. Just remember: in the words of Aaliyah, if at first you don't succeed, dust yourself off and try again.

---

*"Do not fear, for I have redeemed you; I have called you by name, you are mine. When you pass through the waters, I will be with you; and through the rivers, they shall not overwhelm you; when you walk through fire you shall not be burned, and the flame shall not consume you. For I am the Lord your God, the Holy One of Israel, your Savior" (Isaiah 43:1-3). Every praise is to our God. Every word of worship with one accord. We sing hallelujah to our God, Glory Hallelujah is to our God. God's my savior, God's my healer, God's my deliverer, yes he is! (Hezekiah Walker, "Every Praise.")*

---

*Chapter Sixteen*

# CLIMBING THE MOUNTAIN!

***The meaning of the number 16 is always giving you hope that even amid challenges and problems, you will always emerge victorious.***

As I write this in 2022, my business following is going up! I am continually climbing the mountain. A large part of that includes exploring new ideas and reaching more people.

One of our latest successes is our KKW vending machine. My friend, Nakisha, likes to research and come up with new ideas. She called me one day from work on her break and said, "Hey, I've got an idea. And I think that you should do it, but if you don't wanna do it, you don't have to do it. It might sound kind of crazy. I think that you should get your own vending machine. You can put all your products in it."

I thought about it, and said, "If I had a vending machine, I could add all of my paper and supplies. And then I could put it in front of my store, so that when I'm closed, people could still get their items."

Immediately, I started scrolling, looking for a vending machine, and then I found one. Before I paid for it, I was able to customize it with our KKW logo and the sizes for the items I wanted. Three months later when it arrived from China custom-made, I placed it in front of our store.

We sized it to fit all four sizes of sublimation paper in the machine. In the process of the machine being made, we changed the design of the packaging for the paper from plastic to cardboard. Now, the machine can only hold the smaller sizes. It worked out because those are the most popular sizes and tend to sell the fastest. People use their credit card or phone app to purchase items from the vending machine. While the glass is shatterproof, I'm not worried about people breaking into it. I have cameras out front of the store. Most people wouldn't try to break in because there's no cash in it, and unless you know about sublimation, you can't use the products inside of it.

The machine is really bright and has a bunch of bright, neon colors. You can see it from a mile away! Part of the machine includes a video screen with a commercial of me talking about my products that plays nonstop. My clients often use the vendor machine, and they love it. Once a month, I restock all the materials.

Once, the camera outside my building caught a video at the machine. A little boy made his dad drive him to the vending machine. And when he pulled up, the camera picked up on the boy who said, "I'm gonna go get my money."

And his dad said, "For what? You can't use any of this stuff."

They argued until the dad told his son the item he wanted costs $19.

The little boy suddenly said, "Oh, I don't have that."

I caught it all on camera, and when I watched it, I cracked up laughing.

In addition to new ideas like the vending machine, I've been changing my business strategy. When I started KKW in my house, it was a big deal when I expanded to an office space. Now, I am feeling called to reach out to other areas, not just through the internet but in person, too. You might be surprised, dear reader, to learn that, in the beginning, I was not very confident in myself and my business. While I was experiencing financial success, I didn't think anyone noticed the business I was building. I was building a presence on social media, but I didn't know if anyone outside my group was paying attention.

In late 2021, I decided to get myself noticed and put my business out there, to let people know that I'm here and who I am. In the early months of 2022, I traveled to decorated apparel expos in Kansas City, Missouri, and Atlantic City, New Jersey. I wasn't sure what to expect when I arrived and set my mind to focus on meeting new people. To my surprise, when I arrived in Kansas City, I found out that people already knew who I was. And even better, they were excited to see me and wanted to be in my presence! Once I arrived at the expo, lots of people wanted to pick my brain about certain things related to sublimation. People had followed me on TikTok—and this was before I went viral. It was really eye-opening when I realized these people knew who I was. Before I arrived, I didn't have any clue that these people knew that I existed.

Soon after my trip to Kansas City, I planned a trip to Atlantic City. One of my employees was supposed to travel with me when suddenly something came up and she was unable to go. Of course, my good friend Nakisha agreed to go, but I knew I needed more help. I reached out to my group members, my followers, and said, "Hey, is anybody able to meet me or go with me to Atlantic City to help me with this expo?"

I wasn't sure what to expect. I was shocked when about ten people reached out. What really got me was when a few people who had never met me agreed to drive from nine and ten hours away. These people didn't know anything about me except that they followed me in my group. I had already rented out a big Airbnb with four bedrooms, so I invited them to drive and meet me there. One lady named Lillian drove north and met me in Virginia and rode with me to Atlantic City. Another lady named Christina drove from Virginia Beach to Atlantic City to help. Several people drove from Philly to help. All of these people who were strangers outside of Nakisha came to support me, and it was absolutely impressive. God always makes a way.

---

Right now, life is so good! I'm continuing to grow a bigger platform. My business has grown. I'm getting known all over. I went viral on TikTok so now I'm able to monetize on that platform. I'm growing from my bootstraps and I'm on the road to billions.

With everybody helping me, my next big milestone on the mountain of success is tackling an upcoming expo in Chicago later in 2022.

Right now, I am dealing with several issues. Recently, I found out I'm going to be going to Chicago by myself because my employee who was supposed to be going had to cancel. Taking a chance, I've reached out to Christina, one of the ladies who came to Atlantic City with me to see if she is able to go. My best friend Brittney said that she can join us, but while I love her, she doesn't know anything about sublimation. People come to these events to gain knowledge of information concerning their business. It's going to be kind of hard. Even with my best friend there, since she doesn't know about sublimation, I'm still going to basically be doing all the work myself. I'm hoping that the other young lady can come because she is very well versed in sublimation and should be able to answer the questions that people have. I have resellers in Chicago, so they're going to actually come out and help as well.

How it will go in Chicago is a story yet to be told. One thing I know for sure is that I can't do it all by myself. Knowing now that I have strangers who are willing to rally around me and put in that kind of energy into assisting me, especially after I've provided them with the training, is awesome. It's really dope to see it come back full circle. I'm proud to say I've created a beautiful craft community that's like family. I love it here!

---

"I make known the end from the beginning, from ancient times, what is still to come. I say, 'My purpose will stand, and I will do all that I please'" (Isaiah 46:10). "Remember to always be a first-rate version of yourself, instead of a second-rate version of somebody else." —Judy Garland

---

# INTERVIEW QUESTIONS FOR TIFFANY FROM HER FOLLOWERS AND CUSTOMERS

**Q: What do you find most challenging about being a business owner?**

A: The most challenging thing for me about being a business owner is not knowing everything and making huge mistakes that affect my business in a major way. For example, I purchased equipment without completely researching everything that was needed to make the equipment run effectively, causing me to spend a lot of unnecessary money to repair these items.

**Q: What are some difficult obstacles you face when building your business?**

A: Well, where do I start with this question. I went through a lot of trials and tribulations building my brand. I went through numerous employees. The transitions of home businesses to brick and mortar are on another level.

If I could change anything about building my business, I would say that I would research everything and not stop the research until I can tell someone everything about that product's pros and cons. This way, I believe I would be well-versed in my investments and could save some money in the process.

**Q: Would you change anything today about your business knowing as much as you know now about being a business owner?**

A: No, I would not change a thing. I learned, I lost, I cried, I grew! Now, I am a business owner with a product line that is trademarked and has copyrights. I am very proud of myself and my accomplishments thus far.

**Q: What research did you do to ensure your product was high-quality and could stand against competitors in such a highly saturated market?**

A: The research I conducted for my products was tedious; I had samples of different products and I had to physically test them all out to see which one I liked best. I wasted so many substrates (blank items to sublimate on) and wasted so many of the products. Every time I realized it was missing a step in the process, I would go back to my vendors and request they fix that issue, and then I would pay for another set of samples. The upside to this process is that I believe I've created the best sublimation products in the business.

**Q: What made you start this business?**

A: I was getting married and wanted my items customized but within my price range as well, so I decided to learn how to make the items myself and I did. Then, KKW grew from that process, and now, I am the proud owner of a sublimation product line.

**Q: What's next for your brand? Where do you see yourself in the upcoming years?**

A: Next up for KKW are big things that I am currently

manifesting, and I will share them with the world once God brings it to light. In the years to come I see KKW being a household name, and I will be adding new products to my line very soon.

**Q: What do you feel is your biggest accomplishment?**

A: My biggest accomplishment is starting this business and stepping out on faith to put every dollar I had saved to purchase an order for my own brand of sublimation paper. I will never forget that day; it was one of the best days of my life. I place my business in high regard, up there with having children and getting married. So yes, I would say this business is very important to me.

**Q: Was it hard getting your product in Walmart.com?**

A: The short answer is yes, it is a process that I am still currently going through to continue to upload my products to their website. But I would not change the blessing of being on such a huge platform like Walmart.

**Q: What gave you the motivation to keep pushing?**

A: I am a person who does not give up or quit. Therefore, I looked to my higher power and prayed to keep me grounded and to bless me with humbleness, transparency, and the ability to go through this trying process and not give up or give in.

**Q: How does owning a business impact your family?**

A: Owning a business affects my family dynamic in many ways. First, I must say that my time is limited to be spent with family because I am currently trying to build my brand. This leaves me with less time with my husband and children, but they understand the greater goal, which is to give us all a better life. The upside is I can show my children a better life, and they can learn the ways of the business and they can learn to be entrepreneurs like their mother.

**Q: How do you feel you fit in as a Black entrepreneur?**

A: Honestly, I feel like I am an outsider in this business niche market because if you are not in with the "in crowd" then no one wants to be your friend. I understood this before I started KKW, so I learned from other entrepreneurs not in my business niche market. This helped me to see business from different aspects, and I learned that I could build my own place without needing to fit into someone else's box. I also have five college degrees that are focused on business and education, so I am equipped to teach business, and I offer courses on my website.

**Q. What made you write a book about your life?**

A: I decided to write a book about my life to help people by sharing my story. I watched people in my life completely give up due to the loss of loved ones, depression, loss of hope, and much more. After seeing these issues so much, I decided it was time to share my story with the world. I hopefully will help even just one person; that would be awesome.

I hope this book will help the reader to see that life is hard and rewarding at the same time. The reward doesn't come right away but if you stick through it then you will find the pot of gold at the end of the rainbow. Just be patient, and you will see your purpose in life. Once you figure it out, go for it, and don't stop pushing forward.

Good luck! You got this! Go out there and show the world what you got in store for them.

# REFERENCES

**Chapter 1**
Ringling Brothers Barnum & Bailey and are a trademark of RINGLING BROS.-BARNUM & BAILEY COMBINED-SHOWS, INC.

**Chapter 2**
Sprite is a trademark of Coca Cola Company, The

Albuterol (PROAIR HFA (ALBUTEROL SULFATE) INHALATION AEROSOL) is a trademark of Teva Respiratory, LLC.

Wendy's is the trademark of OLDEMARK LLC.

Hooper, Tobe, director. *Poltergeist*. Metro-Goldwyn-Mayer, 1982. 1 hr, 54 min. https://www.imdb.com/title/tt0084516/?ref_=fn_al_tt_1

Vicodin is the trademark of ABBOTT LABORATORIES.

O-B tampons is the trademark of KENDALL COMPANY, THE.

**Chapter 3**

Greyhound is the trademark of GREYHOUND LINES, INC.

Dollar Tree is the trademark of DOLLAR TREE STORES INC.

**Chapter 4**

*A Different World*. 1987-1993. Produced by Carsey-Werner Productions.

*The Cosby Show*. 1984-1992. Produced by Carsey-Werner Productions.

**Chapter 5**

Walmart is the trademark of WAL-MART STORES, INC.

FaceBook is the trademark of Facebook, Inc.

LinkedIn is the trademark of LinkedIn Corporation.

Instagram is the trademark of Instagram, LLC.

Fiverr is the trademark of Fiverr International Ltd.

BREX is the trademark of Brex Inc.

Grainger is the trademark of W. W. GRAINGER, INC.

Uline is the trademark of Uline, Inc.

Quill is the trademark of QUILL LLC.

Wex is the trademark of WEX INC.

Paydex is the trademark of Dun & Bradstreet, Inc.

**Chapter 7**

Bally Total Fitness is the trademark of BALLY TOTAL FITNESS HOLDING CORPORATION.

**Chapter 8**

Cream of Wheat is the trademark of B&G FOODS NORTH AMERICA, INC.

Kurt Carr & The Kurt Carr Singers. "I Almost Let Go." YouTube video. Provided to YouTube by Sony Music Entertainment. Setlist: The Very Best of Kurt Carr & The Kurt Carr Singers. ℗ 2000 Gospocentric. Released on: 2011-12-27, Composer, Lyricist, Producer: Kurt Car, Auto-generated by YouTube. https://www.youtube.com/watch?v=0orieg6PZ2I

**Chapter 9**

Girl Scouts is the trademark of GIRL SCOUTS OF THE UNITED STATES OF AMERICA.

Google is the trademark of GOOGLE LLC.

**Chapter 10**

Sallie Mae is the trademark of SALLIE MAE BANK.

James Fortune & FIYA. "I Trust You."CoCo Brother Presents Gospel Mix V. Licensed to YouTube by
MNRK Music Group (on behalf of Blacksmoke Worldwide Music); LatinAutor - SonyATV, CD Baby Sync Publishing, LatinAutorPerf, ASCAP, UNIAO BRASILEIRA DE EDITORAS DE MUSICA - UBEM, Polaris Hub AB, and 11

Music Rights Societies. https://www.youtube.com/watch?v=rRwQy2eQbJM&list=RDrRwQy2eQbJM&start_radio=1

**Chapter 11**
Kustom Kreationz is the trademark of Kustom Kreationz, LLC.

Yolanda Adams. "The Battle Is the Lord's." Save The World ℗ 1993 Diadem Music Group, Inc., a Music Entertainment Group Co. Released on: 1997-03-3. Composer, Lyricist: V. Michael McKay, Producer: Ben Tankard, Auto-generated by YouTube. https://www.youtube.com/watch?v=TulOY7XlF8A

**Chapter 13**
Facebook is the trademark of Facebook, Inc.

PayPal is the trademark of PAYPAL, INC.

American Express and Plum Card are trademarks of American Express Marketing & Development Corp.

Dun & Bradstreet is the trademark of THE DUN & BRADSTREET CORPORATION.

*Shark Tank*. 2009 to present. Produced by Mark Burnett Productions (2009–11), One Three Media (2012–14), United Artists Media Group (2014–15), MGM Television (2016–), Sony Pictures Television Studios.

FUBU is the trademark of GTFM, INC.

Bed, Bath and Beyond is the trademark of LIBERTY PROCUREMENT CO. INC.

Michaels is the trademark of Michaels Stores Procurement Company, Inc.

HSN is the trademark of HSNI, LLC.

Spanx is the trademark of Spanx, Inc.

**Chapter 14**

Amazon is the trademark of Amazon Technologies, Inc.

Walmart is the trademark of WAL-MART STORES, INC.

Michaels is the trademark of Michaels Stores Procurement Company, Inc.

Alibaba is the trademark of Alibaba Group Holding Limited.

**Chapter 15**

Hezekiah Walker. "Every Praise (Radio Edit)." WOW Gospel 2014. Licensed to YouTube by SME (on behalf of RCA Inspiration); Anthem Entertainment (Publishing), LatinAutorPerf, LatinAutor - UMPG, Capitol CMG Publishing, UMPI, ASCAP, Polaris Hub AB, Adorando Brazil, and 12 Music Rights Societie. https://www.youtube.com/watch?v=UuuZMg6NVeA

**Chapter 16**

Judy Garland quote, Goodreads. https://www.goodreads.com/quotes/5466-always-be-a-first-rate-version-of-yourself-and-not

**Interview Questions**

Walmart is the trademark of WAL-MART STORES, INC.

# ABOUT THE AUTHOR

My name is Tiffany Harris, and I am the owner of Kustom Kreationz Wholesale. We specialize in dye sublimation blanks and supplies. Our brick-and-mortar location is in Richmond, Virginia. A little about myself, I am a mother of three, two girls, one boy and one fur baby. I am a wife and a profound businesswoman. I started Kustom Kreationz Wholesale (KKW) because I was getting married and was having issues with people making the customized items I wanted, so I decided to learn how to create them myself. Once I figured out how to make those items I learned about sublimation, and I fell in love. I call myself the Sublimation Diva. I love sublimation and everything about it.

Throughout, my sublimation journey I found there to be issues that were causing me to be delayed in making my products and it really bothered me. I decided to take this huge matter into my own hands and make all my issues and problems with sublimation go away. I started with sublimation paper because I hated all the steps needed to be taken before you could actually press the shirt. For example, if you are pressing a shirt, you must first line the heat press with butcher paper, then line the inside of the shirt with parchment paper, then lint roll the shirt, print the image and then use heat tape and tape the paper down to the shirt. By using KKW we have all but eliminated many of these steps making the process no more than 2 minutes from print to press. With KKW sublimation paper you do not have to use butcher paper, parchment paper, heat tape is optional, and lint rolling is optional but none of these steps are needed. This is when I realized I may have fixed an issue in the sublimation community that most people did not even realize was broken. Next, I decided to make sublimation ink because my customers were having issues securing a great ink option. What I did not know was the affect my paper and ink would have together. I then made my own brand of easy sublitextile, heat tape, and 100% polyester shirts. I originally thought that my paper would be my number one seller and it was until the shirts came into the picture. These shirts are the softest feeling shirts, and they sub so beautifully. If you use my paper, ink, and shirts together it is seriously the holy trinity of sublimation. You will get the best sublimation results EVER! I hope to continue to grow my business and show my many followers that if I can do this they can as well.

www.ingramcontent.com/pod-product-compliance
Ingram Content Group UK Ltd.
Pitfield, Milton Keynes, MK11 3LW, UK
UKHW021649190726
13853UKWH00001B/145